Abstracts of Current Studies

The World Bank Research Program

October 1981

World Bank
1818 H Street, N.W.
Washington, D.C. 20433, U.S.A.

Foreword

This publication provides an overview of the World Bank's research program and a brief description of projects currently in progress.

World Bank research is increasingly conducted in collaboration with researchers and research institutions in developing countries and is focused on problems of mutual concern. Now in its eleventh year, the program is maturing into a network of mutually supportive studies, dealing with general issues of development policy, as well as specific sectoral problems of particular concern to the Bank's operations in developing countries.

By acquainting a wide readership with the studies now under way, the Bank hopes to contribute to a better understanding of the process of development, a crucial element in the effort of international cooperation.

Hollis B. Chenery
Vice President, Development Policy

The Abstracts were compiled, revised, and organized by Nitya Ranjan Pal in the Office of the Research Adviser (Office of the Vice President, Development Policy). Margaret de Tchihatchef edited and produced the booklet.

Contents

Introduction

This compilation of Abstracts provides a summary of work undertaken in the World Bank's central research program.[1] Research has always been an integral part of the Bank's economic work, and the growing diversification of the Bank's lending operations has induced further expansion of research activities.

To give wider dissemination to the results of its research, the Bank now publishes a newsletter, entitled *World Bank Research News*, three times a year. The newsletter supplements the Abstracts by reporting on completed projects, by describing projects that are in the pipeline, not yet included here, and by listing new and forthcoming publications related to the Bank's research. Each issue of *Research News* includes an article that describes various aspects of the Bank's research program in some detail.

The Bank has designed its research program in the light of four major objectives:
- To support all aspects of the World Bank's operations, including the assessment of development progress in member countries.
- To broaden understanding of the development process.
- To improve the Bank's capacity to provide advice to member countries.
- To assist in developing indigenous research capacity in member countries.

To these ends, the World Bank has initiated research projects that develop the data base, construct analytical tools, and extend the Bank's understanding of rural and urban development, industry, trade, economic growth, and social conditions. While the immediate purpose of the research program is to support the Bank's

---

[1]This does not include research related to specific projects, which is funded by loans and credits to member governments and other, generally short-term, studies carried out by the Bank's staff.

own activities, most studies of importance to the operations of the World Bank are relevant to planning and operational agencies in developing countries, as well as to other development finance institutions.

The design and implementation of research can be used to build and strengthen indigenous research capacity in developing countries. The Bank, therefore, stresses collaborative research with individuals and institutes in those countries. Finally, the World Bank's research program may serve to stimulate others to finance studies on topics of particular interest and to improve the coordination of such research.

The Current Research Program

The 102 projects now in the research program are briefly described in this booklet. The studies are grouped into eight functional categories and, within each category, appear in numerical order by reference number. A new series, research applications, has been introduced this year. These essentially are applications of existing research or tried research methodologies to new areas or case studies. Applications are identified by the letter "A" following the reference number of the project and appear in numerical order within each category.

The first category, *Development Policy and Planning,* which is divided into two subsections—"Income Distribution" and "Planning, Growth, and Country Economic Analysis"—represents the core of the Bank's effort to improve country economic analysis. The causes, processes, and consequences of aggregate economic development are analyzed with respect to intersectoral linkages and broad social objectives. Various sophisticated planning and modeling techniques, such as social accounting matrices and general equilibrium and programming models, provide the tools with which issues of structural adjustment facing the developing countries in the 1980s are examined. "The Living Standards Measurement Study" is also to be found in this section.

The second category, *International Finance and Trade,* includes studies that examine the institutional and structural factors underlying changes in the direction of developing countries' trade, particularly in manufactured goods, and their policy implications.

The third category, *Agriculture and Rural Development,* focuses on the design of rural development strategies, particularly on the role of the small farmer and the problems of channeling funds and distributing food to the rural poor. Some studies address planning and policy aspects of agricultural development, such as the design and operation of irrigation projects and the role of technical and financial services in the adoption of agricultural innovations. Others consider the consequences of risk for agricultural policy and the impact of rural development on employment.

The fourth category, *Industry*, is concerned with the sources and patterns of industrial growth and with initiating policies and techniques for efficient industrial development. The use of programming techniques for sector analysis and project design is studied, as are issues of appropriate technology in the manufacturing sector. Also included in this category are studies on the managerial characteristics of public enterprises and the evolution of small-scale enterprises.

The fifth category has been expanded to cover *Transportation, Water, and Telecommunications*, making the classification of the Abstracts consistent with the one now used in the Bank's project work. Research in this category is concerned with the design, implementation, and management of transportation, water supply, and sanitation systems. Of special importance in this section are the studies on highway design and maintenance and on identifying appropriate technologies and pricing policies for urban services.

Research on *Energy*, which now comprises the sixth category, includes the study of tools for analyzing investment policies in the energy sector and the pricing of indigenous energy resources.

Studies in the seventh category, *Urbanization and Regional Development*, seek to improve understanding of the spatial and economic effects of policy intervention in cities of the developing world. One project develops a framework for the analysis of public finance in metropolitan areas, while another studies the characteristics of housing markets.

The eighth category, *Population and Human Resources*, comprises three main fields—"Education," "Labor and Employment," and "Population and Health." Studies on education are evaluating the efficacy of alternative modes of transmission (for example, educational radio) and measuring the impact of education on productivity, employment, and incomes. The labor market studies focus on the informal urban sector and its relation to rural-urban migration. The studies on population consider the determinants of fertility and the economics of household size; those on health, the influence of augmented food intake and efficient disease control on workers' nutrition and productivity.

This year's Abstracts do not include projects completed before October 1981. The few projects completed thereafter are listed in the current edition of this booklet to mark their progress toward the dissemination of results.

Correspondence

Requests for information on specific research projects in progress should be addressed to the Director of the responsible World Bank department listed in the Abstracts. The completion date is only an estimate.

Reports of the World Bank released for general distribution are listed in *The World Bank Catalog of Publications,* which provides detailed ordering instructions. The Catalog may be obtained by writing to:

> World Bank
> Publications Distribution Unit
> 1818 H Street, N.W.
> Washington, D.C. 20433, U.S.A.

> World Bank
> European Office
> 66, avenue d'Iéna
> 75116 Paris, France

Copies of the reports for general release, listed at the end of some of the Abstracts, may also be ordered from the two above addresses, unless otherwise stated.

It should be noted that studies that have been published by an outside publisher cannot be obtained from the Bank. These publications are available in bookstores or may be ordered from the publisher indicated. The Catalog includes a list of external publishers of World Bank material and their agents worldwide.

Other information concerning the Bank's research may be obtained from the Secretary to the Research Committee, Office of the Vice President, Development Policy, World Bank.

List of Abstracts of Current Studies, by Functional Category

1. Development Policy and Planning

1-A. Income Distribution

1-B. Planning, Growth, and Country Economic Analysis

2. International Finance and Trade

3. Agriculture and Rural Development

4. Industry

5. Transportation, Water, and Telecommunications

6. Energy

7. Urbanization and Regional Development

8. Population and Human Resources

8-A. Education

8-B. Labor and Employment

8-C. Population and Health

1
Development Policy and Planning
1–A. Income Distribution

The Living Standards Measurement Study

Ref. No. 600–07

The Living Standards Measurement Study (LSMS) is designed to develop better methods of measuring living standards and how they change over time. Even in countries with quite advanced statistical systems, the evaluation of past development experience and the formulation of future policies to alleviate poverty are handicapped by a lack of systematic knowledge about the living standards of different socioeconomic groups within the population. The LSMS is a response to this situation and will draw on the Bank's experience in research on income distribution and in the technical assistance that research staff have given in the design and analysis of income distribution data.

The study emphasizes the data that are needed to monitor and evaluate development experience, and how these data can be used. Methods of data collection and problems of survey design will be important components of the study, but only insofar as they are essential to find out which groups in society are benefiting from the development process and which, if any, are being left outside it. In addressing these primary questions, the LSMS will be concerned with consumption and income levels, household composition, and sources of income. The connections between income distribution and the production structure will receive particular attention.

The ultimate objective of the study, which is to be completed in 1984, is to define a relatively simple set of household surveys and other instruments that can be set within a country's national statistical framework and whose results can be readily processed and interpreted. Designing these instruments should help make data on living standards internationally more comparable, although the general concepts will always require adaptation to particular national conditions and requirements. Thus, the experiments that are part of LSMS will be conducted in a variety of countries and adapted to their needs. In initial informal discussions, several national statistical authorities have responded enthusiastically to the possibility of collaborating in this experimental work.

As a research study, LSMS is being conducted to encourage debate and exchanges of scientific opinion. The International Statistical Institute in the Netherlands and the International Association on Income and Wealth, New Haven (Connecticut), are providing strong support by including the topics that concern LSMS on the agenda of their future meetings, and in other ways. The study has its own series of working papers, which is freely available on request. This series started with papers presented at a meeting of experts in February 1980; subsequent papers reporting on the interim results of the study are now being prepared, and the series will continue with papers presented at an LSMS conference held in Warwick, United Kingdom.

The study has three phases. Phase I started with an evaluation of existing data and methods for their collection, much of which is already completed as reflected in the papers contributed to the Expert Group Meeting mentioned earlier. This work is proceeding with analyses of selected data sets which can usefully complement what is known already. Phase I will then continue with the design of new survey models and appropriate pretests both of subject treatment and experiments of a more purely statistical character. Since the ultimate purpose of LSMS is to provide a data base useful for policy formulation, the work on the design of the surveys and testing will be related directly to the preliminary design of various topical studies, each of which corresponds to an area of policy. So far, six topics have been identified: income distribution and national accounts; demand analysis; poverty and inequality; manpower, employment, and earnings; economic influences on demography; and access to public services. The data needs of these studies will define the content of survey questionnaires and modules.

Phase II of LSMS will include all the field work. It will overlap in time with Phase I and Phase III, not least to allow revision of the survey modules and the topical studies. It is proposed to go beyond pretests and participate in full surveys in five or six countries.

The data collected in Phase II will provide the empirical basis for analysis in Phase III. This phase will range from initial data processing to completion of the topical studies. It will be concerned with the management of microdata sets in participating countries, so as to allow easy retrieval and flexibility of access, and with the design of tabular and graphical forms for presentation of the results. Ultimately, the emphasis will be on using the data to extract policy implications. Next to the analytical studies, the output of Phase III will include survey questionnaires and detailed manuals on survey design and field work. Guidelines for local adaptation based on the LSMS experience will be included. Lastly, the data collected are likely to be rich enough to allow a number of specialized investigations outside of the scope of the six topical studies. Such investigations will be reported in scientific papers published in the LSMS Working Paper Series.

Responsibility: Development Research Center—F. Graham Pyatt, William P. McGreevey, and Christiaan N. Grootaert. A large number of Bank staff from operational and research departments will collaborate on this project.

The complexity of the project calls for contributions from a wide range of consultants. A number of national statistical agencies and others have offered to support the project and collaborate in all phases. Specific arrangements are being developed.

Completion date: Phase I—December 1981; Phase II—June 1983; Phase III—December 1984.

Reports

Pyatt, F. Graham. "Some Conceptual Problems of Measuring Living Standards, or: How Do We Find Out Who is Benefiting from Development?" Paper presented at the meeting of the International Statistical Institute, Manila, Philippines, December 1979.
"LSMS Program Description." September 1981.
LSMS Working Papers Nos. 1–10:
  1. Chander, Ramesh; Grootaert, Christiaan N.; and Pyatt, F. Graham. "Living Standards Surveys in Developing Countries."
  2. Visaria, Pravin. "Poverty and Living Standards in Asia:

An Overview of the Main Results and Lessons of Selected Household Surveys."

3. Altimir, Oscar, and Sourrouille, Juan. "Measuring Levels
   of Living in Latin America: An Overview of Main
   Problems."

4. United Nations Statistical Office. "Towards More Effec-
   tive Measurement of Levels of Living, and Review of
   Work of the United Nations Statistical Office (UNSO)
   Related to Statistics of Levels of Living."

5. Chander, Ramesh; de André, Paulo T.A.; and Scott,
   Christopher. "Conducting Surveys in Developing Coun-
   tries: Practical Problems and Experience in Brazil,
   Malaysia, and the Philippines."

6. Booker, William; Savane, Landing; and Singh, Parmeet.
   "Household Survey Experience in Africa."

7. Deaton, Angus. "Measurement of Welfare: Theory and
   Practical Guidelines."

8. Mehran, Farhed. "Employment Data for the Measurement of Living Standards."

9. Wahab, Mohammed Abdul. "Income and Expenditure
   Surveys in Developing Countries: Sample Design and
   Execution."

10. Grootaert, Christiaan N., and Saunders, Christopher.
    "Reflections on the LSMS Group Meeting."

Evaluation of Latin American Data on Income Distribution

Ref. No. 670–83

A major limitation of empirical work on income distribution
and the relationship between inequality, poverty, and development is the poor quality of the information that is available. This
study is part of a broad program of work aimed at improving the
data base for the systematic study of distributional problems (see
also "Evaluation of Asian Data on Income Distribution," Ref.
No. 671–08, in this category).

The objectives of this research project are to identify, for each
country in Latin America, a recent data set suitable for the analysis of patterns of income distribution and to use these data to
present a detailed picture of the various aspects of income distribution. Access was obtained to 22 surveys for 11 countries (Ar-

gentina, Brazil, Chile, Colombia, Costa Rica, Ecuador, Honduras, Panama, Peru, Uruguay, and Venezuela). Multiple tabulations of the data have been prepared, accompanied by statements of their basic characteristics. The overall degree of inequality of income will be determined as measured by Lorenz curves and various indices of inequality, such as the Gini coefficient and the Theil index. In addition, the socioeconomic characteristics of different income groups will be identified. An attempt will then be made to examine the validity of various hypotheses about causes of income inequality by examining correlates of inequality in selected surveys.

The final report will also provide an assessment of the quality of the data that are available in Latin America, as well as an evaluation of the degree to which data on income distribution are comparable across countries.

Responsibility: Development Research Center—Pravin Visaria. The project is being undertaken jointly by the World Bank's Development Research Center and the Economic Commission for Latin America (ECLA). The principal researcher is Oscar Altimir, Chief of the ECLA Statistics Division.

Completion date: November 1981.

Reports

The following paper is available from the Development Research Center:

Altimir, Oscar, and Sourrouille, J. "Measuring Levels of Living in Latin America: An Overview of Main Problems." Living Standards Measurement Study (LSMS) Working Paper No. 3. July 1980.

Evaluation of Asian Data on Income Distribution

Ref. No. 671–08

This study was designed to parallel the previous research project, "Evaluation of Latin American Data on Income Distribution," and is part of a work program aimed at improving the data base in this field. The basic research objective was to undertake an analysis of patterns of income distribution for each of the economies of the region.

On the basis of preliminary work, it was decided to concentrate the in-depth analysis of the patterns of income distribution and the nature of poverty on the data sets for India, Malaysia, Nepal, Sri Lanka, and Taiwan. The study has provided profiles of the socioeconomic characteristics of different income groups that are broadly comparable. Particular attention has been paid to the nature of rural-urban differences in income distribution and the relationship between income and various characteristics of the labor force. The project has also provided an assessment of the quality and comparability of available data.

Responsibility: Development Research Center—Pravin Visaria. The study was undertaken jointly with the Economic and Social Commission for Asia and the Pacific (ESCAP). A number of national statistical agencies have provided access to data and, in many cases, have undertaken preliminary data processing.

Completion date: November 1981.

Reports

The following papers are available from the Development Research Center:

Visaria, Pravin. "Demographic Factors and the Distribution of Income: Some Issues." In *Economic and Demographic Change in the 1980s, Proceedings of the Conference of the International Union for the Scientific Study of Population* (held at Helsinki), vol. 1:281–320. Liege, Belgium: IUSSP, 1979. A slightly revised version is available as World Bank Reprint Series: Number 129.
———. "Poverty and Living Standards in Asia." *Population and Development Review* 6 (June 1980).
———. "Poverty and Living Standards in Asia: An Overview of the Main Results and Lessons of Selected Household Surveys." Living Standards Measurement Study (LSMS) Working Paper No. 2. October 1980.

Real Incomes and Economic Welfare of Selected Socioeconomic Groups in Colombia, 1964–78

Ref. No. 672-05

In most respects, Colombia constitutes a case of successful economic development. During the past decade and a half, economic growth has been strong, population growth has declined markedly, and real output per capita has risen by about 4 percent annually. One unknown factor is the extent to which the poor have shared in the benefits of this growth and whether policies for the improvement of the welfare of the poor have been successful.

This research attempts to measure the extent to which different socioeconomic groups among the poorest in Colombia have benefited from growth during the period 1964 to 1978, and to assess the relative importance of the factors contributing to whatever changes have occurred. The study also explores the extent to which poverty is a temporary phase in the life cycle of a large number of families, as opposed to affecting a "hard core" group of families chronically.

The principal objectives of this research are to permit the Bank to direct its lending program more effectively to the poorest groups in the country and to bring renewed attention to welfare and poverty issues in Colombia. A subsidiary objective is that of providing a firmer basis for policy making on welfare and poverty-related matters through an analysis of the relationships between growth and poverty and of the effects on various socioeconomic groups of different policy measures.

This study draws on both macro and micro data to measure relative income movements of various occupational and socioeconomic groups during the period under review. These measurements are compared with the overall growth of income to see how these groups have fared relative to the average.

Four different types of information over time are considered in the interpretation of income and welfare trends. One of these is related to general trends in income distribution, which will be drawn from census and survey data. A second is information on income trends for persons in specific occupational or socioeconomic categories (e.g., workers in manufacturing, services, construction, domestic employment, and so on). Wage data, available from many sources, including industry associations, individual firms, research foundations, and statistical offices, are a third source of information. The fourth is information having to do with career-earning profiles, which will be used in tracing individual earnings and employment through time. There are also several sources relating to consumption and welfare trends (e.g., food consumption and health care, education, health information, and housing). The basic methodology will be to analyze these various sources of data in order to specify the trends that have occurred over the period.

In the 1970s, government policies and development programs in Colombia were directed increasingly to improving the welfare of the poor. The introduction during this period of a national nutrition plan (PAN) and related health programs designed to eliminate malnutrition and raise general health levels was an important advance. The same is true of the integrated rural development (DRI) program to raise agricultural productivity on small farms and assist in the extension of services to rural areas.

In addition, health and education programs directed toward the poor have been expanded, water and sewerage services have been extended to numerous low-income areas, low-cost housing has been provided on an increased scale, and family planning services have been made available to a rising proportion of Colombian families. Tax reforms, price controls, and subsidized public transport services all have been aimed at improving the lot of the poorest. Other than a study by Marcelo Selowsky in 1974, which dealt with a few of these issues, only limited attempts have been made to evaluate the individual or joint effects of these policies and programs on the welfare of the poor. The present study is intended to fill the gap.

Responsibility: Latin America and the Caribbean Country Programs Department II—George R. Gebhart and Frederick Z. Jaspersen. Miguel Urrutia, Director of the Fundación para la Educación Superior y el Desarrollo (FEDESARROLLO), Bogota, played a major role in the research design and is responsible for executing the study. Richard Webb collaborated in the project design before leaving the Bank.

Completion date: November 1981.

1–B. Planning, Growth, and Country Economic Analysis

International Comparison Project

Ref. Nos. 670–68 and 671–91

The International Comparison Project (ICP) is a cooperative

effort, begun in 1968 under the aegis of the United Nations, to establish a reliable system of comparisons of real product and the purchasing power of currencies. The World Bank joined the ICP in 1969 and has been a major supporter since that time. In addition to the United Nations and the World Bank, the Ford Foundation and a number of governments have made direct contributions to the work; every participating country has contributed significantly by providing resources for collecting data on its own economic activity.

The ICP has two main objectives: first, to work out the methods required for a system of international comparisons and, second, to apply these methods to a gradually expanding sample of countries with the intention of eventually establishing global coverage. The project has advanced in well-defined stages. In Phase I, the results of which were published in 1975, the essential features of the methodology were formulated and detailed comparisons were produced for 10 countries, varying significantly in type, stage of development, and location, for the year 1970 (and for six countries for 1967 as well). The Phase II report, published in 1978, added six countries, including four developing countries, to the original 10, and included estimates for 1973 as well as 1970. In the final phase of the study (Phase III), the list of countries covered has been expanded to 34 and the entire data base has been updated to 1975. More than half of the countries covered in the final stage are developing countries.

The project has produced a set of price and per capita quantity comparisons for gross domestic product (GDP), its three main expenditure subaggregates (consumption, investment, and government), and 36 major components for each country and year covered. These estimates are not subject to excessive revision when additional countries are added; they are both base-country invariant and transitive, characteristics which were established, at the outset of the study, as being highly desirable. The underlying detailed data are provided in the reports to enable researchers to aggregate the quantity data in ways of their own choice.

Work on the initial research phase of the ICP was concluded with the completion of the Phase III study and the associated data base for 34 countries in June 1981. The final report will be published in early 1982. With support provided under research project Ref. No. 671–91, arrangements have been completed for transfer of the basic work on the ICP on a permanent basis to the United Nations Statistical Office. The benchmark estimates will be kept up to date, and additional countries will be brought into the data base. Under Phase IV, which began in 1980 under UN auspices, comparisons will be made for some 60–65 countries, including most of the countries covered in Phase III, with new countries concentrated primarily in Africa, Asia, and Latin America.

Responsibility: Economic Analysis and Projections Department—Robert A. McPheeters, Jr. Professor Irving B. Kravis, University of Pennnsylvania, is Director of the project; Hughes Picard, United Nations Statistical Office, is ICP Unit Director at the United Nations.

Completion date: Phase III—November 1981.

Reports

Heston, Alan. "A Comparison of Some Short-Cut Methods of Estimating Real Product per Capita." *The Review of Income and Wealth* 19 (March 1973):79–104.

Kravis, Irving B.; Heston, Alan; and Summers, Robert. "International Comparison of Real Product and its Composition: 1950–77." University of Pennsylvania Discussion Paper No. 405. December 24, 1979. Published in *The Review of Income and Wealth* (March 1980):19–66.

————. *Phase II: International Comparisons of Real Product and Purchasing Power.* Baltimore and London: The Johns Hopkins University Press, 1978.

————. *Phase III: World Product and Income: International Comparisons of Real GDP.* Baltimore and London: The Johns Hopkins University Press, 1982 (forthcoming).

————. "Real GDP per Capita for More than 100 countries." *The Economic Journal* (June 1978).

————. "The Role of Regionalization in a Worldwide System of International Product Comparisons." Paper prepared for a Conference on Purchasing Power and Real Product Comparisons at the Economic Commission for Europe, Geneva, Switzerland, May 1979.

Kravis, Irving B.; Kenessey, Zoltan; Heston, Alan; and Summers, Robert. *Phase I: A System of International Comparisons of Gross Product and Purchasing Power.* Baltimore and London: The Johns Hopkins University Press, 1975.

Summers, Robert. "International Price Comparisons Based Upon Incomplete Data." *The Review of Income and Wealth* 19 (March 1973):1-16.

A complete bibliography, covering the main ICP research reports, status and planning reports, documentation and manuals for data collection, and miscellaneous reports and studies, most of which have been published, is available from the Economic Analysis and Projections Department, World Bank.

Prototype Models for Country Analysis

Ref. No. 670-86

The World Bank devotes substantial time and resources to models for country economic analysis. In recent years, major advances have been made by establishing a systematic quantitative underpinning to the Bank's projections of external capital requirements and also by attaining a degree of uniformity in the quantitative procedures applied to a large number of countries. About a decade has passed since the conceptual basis for these first-generation models was established, and, in that time, the art of applied model building has improved considerably. Moreover, revised model frameworks are necessary, because (1) the Bank and its member governments have a heightened interest in the distributive aspects of economic growth and development policy (e.g., the emphasis on the incidence of taxation and public expenditure and not just on the size of the budget); (2) an expanding data base in most countries can be utilized for more realistic models; and (3) new computational procedures allow models to be constructed much more quickly than before.

The purpose of this research project is to explore the possibility of developing quantitative frameworks that address a broader range of issues in development policy, including the effects of alternative development strategies on employment creation and income distribution, the traditional/modern production dichotomy, and problems of investment allocation. The models are also being designed to benefit from cross-section data and to include more specific policy instruments.

The first phase of the project involved a careful review of the experience of others in building and using economywide models. It emphasized the pioneering efforts to make prices and incomes endogenous in computable multisectoral or multiproduct models, especially the work of Leif Johansen and the CHAC model ("The Agricultural Sector in Mexico," Ref. No. 670-16, a recently completed study).

The second phase of the project has involved designing optimal model specifications and establishing their properties and data requirements. The third and final phase, which is currently under way, involves pilot applications of several models to the Republic of Korea. A number of reports have been published on the work so far; a manuscript is being prepared as the final product of the study.

Responsibility: Development Research Center—Roger D. Norton.

Completion date: November 1981.

Reports

Candler, Wilfred V., and Norton, Roger D. "Multi-Level Programming." DRC Discussion Paper No. 20. World Bank: Development Research Center, January 1977.

―――. "Multi-Level Programming and Development Policy." World Bank Staff Working Paper No. 258. May 1977.

Hong, Seok Hyun. "A Model for Analyzing the Incidence of Fiscal Policy in Korea." Ph.D. Dissertation, Stanford University, February 1980.

Inman, R.A.; Kim, Yoon Hyung; and Norton, Roger D. "A Multi-Sectoral Model with Endogenous Terminal Conditions." *Journal of Development Economics* (June 1979).

Norton, Roger D., and Scandizzo, Pasquale L. "A Computable Class of General Equilibrium Models." DRC Discussion Paper No. 24. World Bank: Development Research Center, May 1977.

―――. "Market Equilibrium Computations in Activity Analysis Models." *Operations Research* (1980).

Norton, Roger D., and Thee, Seung Yoon. "A Macroeconometric Model of Inflation and Growth in South Korea." In W. Cline and S. Weintraub (eds.), *Economic Stabilization in Developing Countries.* Washington, D.C.: The Brookings Institution, 1980.

Social Accounts and Development Models

Ref. No. 671-27

Macroeconomic analysis of the development process has been

restricted mainly to two-gap models of resource needs and input-output models of industrial structure. This framework is inadequate for studying policies that deal with problems of employment generation, income redistribution, and eradication of poverty. This study attempts to provide a basis for macroeconomic models, which permits analysis of the trade-offs between alternative policy goals. The analysis focuses simultaneously on the causes of poverty and inequality and on their measurement, and on the determination of both prices and quantities in a model framework. The study involves an attempt to construct a social accounting matrix (SAM) for Malaysia and to develop an economywide model based on the SAM.

Data needs are identified on the basis of the United Nations system of standardized national accounts, which presents annual data in a SAM framework. Since the UN system imposes a heavy burden on the statistical offices of developing countries, the research begins with specific country studies on the feasibility of obtaining basic data in modified versions of the UN format. At the same time, some extensions of the standardized UN system are required to encompass questions of income distribution, employment, basic needs, and poverty in an integrated framework. Systems of classification (e.g., the level of disaggregation) and methods of reconciling data from various sources are studied in order to make the system more relevant for planning.

The elaboration of data requirements is paralleled by research on model structures within the SAM framework. The model being developed generalizes the linear (input-output) models by allowing for price substitution. Through extensive use of CES functions, the basic model provides a general and flexible framework that includes a wide range of existing models as special cases. A major feature is the specification of two-way causal links between income distribution and the structure of production, both of which are endogenous.

A conference has been held as part of the project, bringing together a number of individuals with practical experience in SAM construction and applications. The papers delivered at this conference will be published in a volume, and two further volumes are being drafted on the specific work on Malaysia.

Responsibility: Development Research Center—F. Graham Pyatt, with the assistance of Jefferey Round and Frank Lysy (consultants). The Department of Statistics and the Economic Planning Unit of Malaysia have been closely involved in the work.

Completion date: December 1981.

A General Algebraic Modeling System (GAMS)

Ref. No. 671–58

Mathematical modeling has developed into one of the major tools of strategic planning. Its potential power and relevance in sectoral and economywide applications have been demonstrated convincingly over the last decade in a research-oriented environment. Despite this general acceptance, few mathematical models are being built outside the research laboratory. Many problems can be attributed to the current approach to model building, which requires a variety of technical skills and which fails to address problems of documentation, communication, and dissemination of mathematical models. The existing solution algorithms also have input requirements that are not compatible with each other; this results in different representations of the same model.

The project explores a machine-intensive route to modeling, and aims at a dramatic reduction in the time needed to develop a model, in the technical skills required, and in the total cost associated with existing modeling and data systems. GAMS is a system that provides a formal framework for the specification, manipulation, generation, and reporting of models and their associated data.

The two main components of GAMS are the definition of a uniform notation (formal language) to allow unambiguous representations of models and data and a modeling system that automatically analyzes and translates models from one representation into another, as required by different solution processes.

A number of large-scale models developed in the World Bank are used as test cases and form the nucleus of a uniform model library. The series, The Planning of Investment Programs (see "Programming in the Manufacturing Sector," Ref. No. 670–24, in category 4. Industry), has adopted the GAMS representation to guarantee consistency and replicability of all models and their data throughout the series.

Phase I of the project concentrated on language definitions, the integration of a relational data base into the system, and the automatic interface to commercial linear programming systems.

The program is now in Phase II which has been developed on the basis of responses and recommendations from users. The major thrust is in the area of large nonlinear models that utilize new concepts in automatic recognition of structures and the facilities of an extended data base.

Responsibility: Development Research Center—Alexander Meeraus, in collaboration with Johannes J. Bisschop, Arne Drud, David Kendrick, Leon Lasdon, and Paul van der Eijk (consultants).

Completion date: December 1981.

Reports

Bisschop, J., and Meeraus, A. "On the Development of a General Algebraic Modeling System in a Strategic Planning Environment." In *Mathematical Programming Studies* (forthcoming).

———. "Matrix Augmentation and Partitioning in the Updating of the Basis Inverse." *Mathematical Programming*, vol. 13, no. 3.

———. "Matrix Augmentation and Structure Preservation in Linearly Constrained Control Problems." *Mathematical Programming*, vol. 18, no. 1.

———. "Selected Aspects of a General Algebraic Modeling Language." In *Proceedings of the 9th IFIPS Conference on Optimization*. Berlin and Heidelberg: Springer Verlag, 1980.

———. "Towards Successful Modeling Applications in a Strategic Planning Environment." In G. Dantzig, M. Dempsler, and M. Kellio, (eds.), *Large-Scale Linear Programming*. Vienna: International Institute for Applied Systems Analysis, 1981.

Lasdon, L., and Meeraus, A. "Solving Nonlinear Economic Planning Models Using GRG Algorithms." In *Proceedings of the International Symposium of Systems Optimization and Analysis*. Berlin and Heidelberg: Springer Verlag, 1979.

A Series of Technical Notes (currently 20) that addresses specific issues related to the development of GAMS is available from the Development Research Center.

Small-Enterprise Financing: The Role of Informal Credit Markets

Ref. No. 671-65

In many developing countries, particularly in Asia and Africa, the majority of small enterprises is financed by so-called informal credit markets which have links with both the financial institutions and the corporate sector. In spite of their significance, these credit markets have not been studied adequately so far; most of the information available is of an impressionistic nature. The study of their functioning is useful in several ways:

1. It could ascertain whether the real cost of lending (administrative cost plus default risk) in these markets differs significantly from that in the formal financial markets.
2. It could suggest how these markets may be linked with the formal financial structure for the provision of productive credit at reasonable social cost to small enterprises in agriculture, industry, and trade.
3. It could indicate policy measures essential for regulating speculative activities in real estate and commodity markets.
4. It could suggest ways of inducing these indigenous institutions to evolve into modern, viable financial enterprises.

The specific objective of this research is to study, on a pilot basis, the functioning of one significant element of the informal credit markets in India, namely the Shroffs. The Shroffs are indigenous bankers who, like banks in the organized sector, extend and create credit through the issue of indigenous bills of exchange as well as other credit instruments. The funds lent are drawn from their own capital, from public deposits, from loans from other Shroffs, and even loans from commercial banks.

The aspects of the methods by which the Shroffs function that have been investigated are:

1. Their sources of funds and the terms related to each source.
2. The pattern of their credit allocation to small enterprises in trade, agriculture, and industry.
3. The terms and conditions on which credit is provided.
4. The transaction costs (administrative costs plus default risk) of lending to small enterprises.
5. Their links with the formal financial structure.

The results of this research, as well as the completed research on "Korean Informal Markets," are likely to be useful for the policy questions mentioned earlier, which are of interest both to the developing countries and the World Bank. The results are also likely to indicate those aspects of the informal credit markets that need to be studied in depth in India and other countries in

Asia and Africa, such as Indonesia, Kenya, Malaysia, and the Philippines.

The informal nature of these markets generally forecloses random sample surveys, so that the approach of the project has been to conduct in-depth surveys of selected market participants, borrowers, and lenders. The selection involves a considerable amount of judgment and has to be done on a case-by-case basis at the local level. The participants and sources of information are sufficiently dissimilar to provide cross-checks on most of the information obtained. The three consultants engaged in the project have interviewed several hundred informal market participants in Bombay, Calcutta, Madras, Amritsar, Kanpur, and Benares, and in the various commercial centers of Gujarat and South India. The researchers obtained active assistance and cooperation from the associations of Shroffs and brokers, as well as from businessmen and banking and government officials.

The major working hypotheses that emerge from the two studies on informal markets are:

1. The informal markets constitute a significant element of the capital markets in some developing countries.
2. The relationship between the formal and informal markets is both competitive and complementary.
3. The informal market dealers are able to compete effectively with the banks in certain segments of the capital markets as their financial technology is different from that of the banks, which results in lower transaction costs for lenders and borrowers.
4. Legal restrictions on the markets are counterproductive as they merely tend to raise transaction costs of dealers and their customers.
5. Interest rates in both markets move together; hence a policy of "high" interest rates would not be effective in integrating the two markets.
6. Effective ways of integrating the two markets appear to be: (a) enlarging the geographical and functional scope of the banking systems through an appropriate change in their financial technology and (b) linking the two markets through lending by banks to the informal market dealers.

Responsibility: Development Economics Department—Vinayak V. Bhatt directs the research, which is carried out by Professor

Thomas A. Timberg, Ramaswami Krishnan of the Reserve Bank of India, and C. V. Aiyar of the Union Bank of India (consultants).

Completion date: November 1981.

Reports

The following studies are available from the Public Finance Division, Development Economics Department:

Aiyar, C.V. "Small Enterprise Financing: The Role of Informal Credit Markets: A Survey." May 1979.

Krishnan, Ramaswami. "Preliminary Report on Informal Credit Markets in India." May 1979.

Park, Yung Chul. "The Unorganized Financial Sector in Korea, 1945–1975." Domestic Finance Studies No. 28. November 1976.

Timberg, Thomas A. "Informal Credit Markets in India." April 1979.

Timberg, Thomas A., and Aiyar, C.V. "Informal Credit Markets in India." Domestic Finance Studies No. 62. May 1980.

Timberg, Thomas A., and Raghavan, V.S. "Notes on Financing Small-Scale Enterprises." Paper presented at the Seminar on Development Bank Management, organized by the World Bank's Economic Development Institute (EDI), Washington, D.C., February 1979.

Research Support for the World Development Report

Ref. No. 671–66

The object of this study is to develop a price-endogenous, interregional model for the world economy, in support of the World Bank's global model of trade and capital flows.

Since 1974, the World Bank has been engaged in global modeling to identify the major constraints affecting the growth of developing countries and to explore alternative strategies for development.

In the Bank's early global modeling work (SIMLINK or Mark I), the problem of describing the interdependence between various parts of the world was simplified by adopting four rather heroic assumptions. The first was that the growth of developing countries was constrained principally by a shortage of foreign exchange. The second was that the availability of foreign exchange depended largely on the industrialized countries, through the impact of their growth on the markets for raw materials and exports of manufactured goods from developing countries, and through their aid policies. The third assumption was that this causal relation was unilateral: developed countries influenced the developing world but there was no feedback. The last assumption was that it was reasonable to divide the countries of the world into four income groups: low-income countries, middle-income countries, oil-exporting developing economies, and developed market economies.

As the SIMLINK framework provided little scope for independent action by the developing countries to improve their situation, other than their efforts at trade promotion, a beginning was made, in 1977, to design a new model.

The Bank's monitoring of problems in developing countries in 1976–77 clearly suggested that the developing world was moving to a situation where many different constraints were at work. The natural way of taking these into account was to introduce all of the alternative constraints into the model as inequalities, thus switching from the set of recursive equations of SIMLINK to a representation of the world economy by linked linear programming models.

The resulting Mark II model, used in the first three editions of the *World Development Report,* is substantially larger than SIM-LINK; it is also far more complex, since a system of linked linear programs is more difficult to manage than a system of recursive equations. The paradigm described by the model is that of a world of closely managed developing economies, whose governments seek the best course of development subject to the constraints on their balance of payments, savings, and industrial capacity.

But this modeling approach raises three interconnected types of problems. The first one is the fundamental question of whether it is appropriate to describe the behavior of developing countries by regional optimizing models. The second is whether the scheme linking the submodels dovetails the components of the system as correctly as possible. The third problem is that of specifying constraints so that the resulting system clearly interprets economic behavior.

The Mark III series of models emerging from the present study is designed to address a number of these problems. Some models have tried to capture the economic realism in a mixed economy where some features of behavior correspond to the competitive equilibrium, while others reflect the existing market rigidities. In either case, the normative decisions of the economic agents play a major role in the mechanics of the solution processes.

In the initial two years of the project (fiscal years 1979 and 1980), the focus was on the construction of the model: basic econometric estimation work, experimentation with the various trial versions of the model, and the streamlining of the solution algorithms. In the third year, which is just coming to an end, Mark III was used extensively in sensitivity runs for the fourth *World Development Report*. In these runs, it explored the mechanics of adjustment between the two cases traced out by the older Mark II model. The two cases are described in detail in the Report. This combination proved to be a useful blend of the two most recent generations of the Bank's global models.

In the coming final year of the project, the focus will be on (1) documentation of the entire system; (2) implementation of a more disaggregated version of Mark III with emphasis on the behavior in the markets for agricultural commodities; and (3) using a version of Mark III in studying the adjustment pattern of developing countries following the first oil-shock of 1973–74, through the use of historical simulations.

Responsibility: Economic Analysis and Projections Department—John D. Shilling and Peter Miovic. The research is being undertaken largely at the Free University of Brussels (Belgium) under the direction of Jean Waelbroeck.

Completion date: June 1982.

Reports:

Carrin, G.; Gunning, J.W.; and Waelbroeck, J. "A General Equilibrium Model for the World Economy: Some Preliminary Results." June 1980 (to appear in B. Hickman, *Global Modelling,* London: Pergamon Press).

Gunning, J. "Rationing in an Open Economy: Fix-Price Equilibrium and Two Gap Models." Center for Econometrics and International Economics (CEME) Working Paper 8002. Free University of Brussels, June 1980.

Waelbroeck, J. "A Global Development Model: the M3 Model of Developing and Developed Countries." Center for Econometrics and International Economics (CEME) Working Paper 7801. Free University of Brussels, 1979.

Growth, Poverty, and Basic Needs: Development Policies in Sri Lanka, Kerala, and Punjab

Ref. No. 671-72

The purpose of this study is to prepare a comparative picture of the course of development in the past quarter century in Sri Lanka and in the states of Kerala and Punjab in India, on the basis of already available information. The analysis of differences in past rates and patterns of growth and development among these three low-income areas should improve understanding of the elements of conflict and complementarity between the growth of overall output and the objectives of poverty eradication, and also furnish some leads for future perspectives and policies in regard to both.

The three cases represent examples in which components of the basic needs basket appear to have been packaged differently and delivered in different sequences and amounts over varied lengths of time. Punjab is at one end of the spectrum, relying primarily upon accelerated economic growth to achieve the alleviation of poverty and the satisfaction of basic needs. Sri Lanka, at the other end, has emphasized direct consumption subsidies and public provision of social services to achieve a fairly high level of the satisfaction of basic needs at low levels of per capita income. Historical and comparative analysis should help to illuminate the nature and magnitude of trade-offs and reinforcements among different basic needs. This knowledge would be useful for designing public policies and projects relating to basic needs in general and in the program and development policy work of the World Bank in the South Asia Region.

The study will blend historical and economic analysis of the development experiences of Sri Lanka and the Indian states of Kerala and Punjab, since the late 1940s. Attempts will be made to isolate distinct segments and sequences of development experience, their policy correlates, developmental inputs, and the relevant indices of performance. Formal statistical techniques for data analysis will be used to the extent possible. The study will attempt to identify observed consequences of known policy interventions and inputs during the quarter century of development experience in each of the three regions.

Responsibility: Development Research Center—Professor B.S. Minhas (consultant).

Completion date: December 1981.

Real Product and World Income Distribution

Ref. No. 671-87

For more than a decade, the World Bank, the United Nations, and a number of governments and private institutions have been engaged in a major effort to develop better means of making international comparisons of income and product in real terms. The research phase of this work, known formally as the International Comparison Project (ICP) (Ref. No. 670-68 in this category), is now coming to a close with the completion of detailed benchmark estimates for 34 countries and the establishment of a permanent program of comparisons in the United Nations Statistical Office. Several important aspects of the ICP methodology, however, require further investigation; this is the primary objective of this research project.

The research covers, in particular, three major areas. The first is a range of problems associated with the use of index numbers in international comparisons. Procedures are being devised to measure, and reduce the effect of, instabilities and intransitivities in the ICP binary system and potential biases in the multilateral system. The second area has to do with the comparative measurement of services in real terms. Problems in this area stem from basic deficiencies in the standard economic accounting systems; these problems spill over into international real income comparisons, where they are frequently exacerbated and may be expected to become even more serious over time. The third area concerns the extension of the benchmark comparisons through various "short-cut" methods. In this area, as well as in the measurement of services, the research is focused on measuring and finding ways to reduce random noise and systematic bias in the ICP system and derived short-cut estimates and, thus, to improve the quality and credibility of the data.

An important objective of the project is to create a body of real income estimates for a large number of countries and over a considerable number of years. Improvements will be incorporated in the data base and in the methodology for an extended coverage emerging from the concentrated statistical analysis of the system in the three areas outlined above. This expanded data base is expected to become an increasingly important source of information for the analysis of long-term growth patterns and changes in the structure of global income distribution. Consequently, the project also provides for application of the extended data to the study of patterns of development, with particular emphasis on nonlinear models of economic growth based on a moving cross-section of countries at different levels of development.

Responsibility: Economic Analysis and Projections Department—John D. Shilling. The research is being carried out by Professor Robin L. Marris (consultant).

Completion date: November 1981.

Reports

Marris, Robin L. "Catch-up, Slow Down or Convergence? Statistical Observations on 25 Years of World Economic Growth in the Light of Kravis Numbers." World Bank: Economic Analysis and Projections Department, March 1980.

_____. "A Cross-sectional Econometric Model for Explaining Growth Rates of Real GDP per Capita in Various Classes of Developing and Industrial Countries" (draft). World Bank: Economic Analysis and Projections Department, July 1981.

_____. "Real Domestic Product, Purchasing Power, Exchange Rates, Comparative Inflation Rates and Related Data, for One Hundred Countries 1950–1978." World Bank: Economic Analysis and Projections Department, May 1980.

_____. "The Sensitivity of Real Product Estimates to Assumptions about Service Outputs." World Bank: Economic Analysis and Projections Department, June 1980.

_____. "The Services Sector: Alternative Measurements in Theory and Practice." Paper prepared for a United Nations Conference on the Treatment of Services in International Real Product Comparisons, Bellagio, Italy, December 1980.

_____."A Survey and Critique of World Bank Supported Research on International Comparisons of Real Product." World Bank Staff Working Paper No. 365. December 1979.

Marris, Robin L., and Theil, Henri. "International Comparisons of Economic Welfare." Paper prepared for a joint meeting of the American Economic Association and the Association for Comparative Economic Studies, Denver, Colorado, September 1980.

Research Dissemination: A Computable General Equilibrium Model of Turkey

Ref. No. 672-04

In recent years, the World Bank has sponsored a number of research projects to improve the specification of multisector, economywide models for studying a variety of issues in developing countries. In particular, a model of Turkey has been developed that focuses on issues of growth, trade policy, and industrial structure. This model is in the family of computable general equilibrium (CGE) models. It is highly nonlinear and determines product prices, factor prices, and the exchange rate endogenously so as to clear the markets for commodities, labor, and foreign exchange. Market clearing is achieved by a variation in prices, which equates supply and demand in the various markets, while the behavior of the different "actors" in the economy—producers, consumers, government, and the rest of the world—is specified separately. In the Turkey application, a version of the model was specified in which the exchange rate was fixed and the adjustment to foreign payments imbalances was made through economywide import rationing by means of import premia that equilibrate the market for foreign exchange. The model has been used for a variety of reports within the Bank. It has also provided projections that aided in policy analysis for the report of the Special Economic Mission to Turkey in April 1979.

The development and application of CGE models has aroused interest in a number of academic and policy-making institutions in developing countries. This research project was initiated in response to a request from the Institute of Economic and Social Research at the Middle East Technical University, Ankara, to acquire the CGE modeling framework developed for the Bank's model of Turkey. The goal of the project is to transfer the modeling technology, including the computer program, to the group in Ankara. Their stated intention is: (1) to develop a local modeling capacity that will enable them to prepare policy-conditional forward projections for the Turkish economy and (2) to embark on more detailed empirical studies of particular topics based on the overall model framework.

Responsibility: Development Economics Department and *Europe, Middle East, and North Africa Projects Department II—* Sherman Robinson and Jayanta Roy, respectively, in collaboration with Merih Celasun, Middle East Technical University, Ankara.

Completion date: December 1981.

Reports

Celasun, Merih. "Extension of the Data Base for the Sources of Growth: Study on the Turkish Economy." Mimeo. Ankara: Middle East Technical University, May 1981.

Dervis, Kemal, and Robinson, Sherman. "The Foreign Exchange Gap, Growth and Industrial Strategy in Turkey: 1973–1983." World Bank Staff Working Paper No. 306. November 1978.

Dubey, Vinod; Faruqi, Shakil; et al. "Turkey: Policies and Prospects for Growth." World Bank: Europe, Middle East, and North Africa Regional Office, March 1980.

Reduced Information Methods of International Real Income Comparisons

Ref. No. 672-16

It is generally recognized that intercountry comparisons of relative levels of income should be carried out with national income converted to a common currency using purchasing power parity (PPP) instead of exchange rates. Unfortunately, reliable estimates of PPPs are available for only a handful of countries because the standard benchmark method of estimating them requires a very substantial commitment of time and resources.

With financial support from the World Bank, the International Comparison Project (ICP) (see Ref. No. 670–68 in this category) has, in three phases extending over 12 years, produced PPP estimates for 34 countries and laid the foundation for developing a worldwide system of real income comparisons. During Phase IV, ending in 1985, the ICP expects to extend coverage to over 60 countries.

The amount of time and resources required for a full-scale

comparison of the ICP type is so large that a system of comparison covering all countries of the world is regarded as infeasible. Attempts have been made to use shortcut methods that seek to predict real incomes on the basis of some physical or monetary indicators. The World Bank has been funding research in this direction also—for example, through the research project "Real Product and World Income Distribution" (Ref. No. 671–87 in this category). But shortcut estimates, although good on the average, are found to have unacceptably large residual errors for individual countries. It is now apparent that in order to succeed in developing a truly universal system of real income comparisons, a reduced information method must be found that will produce real income comparisons quickly and cheaply with much less than the full set of price and expenditure information currently required by the ICP.

This research project is designed to investigate various approaches to reduced information estimates, with a view to finding one that will enable the ICP at the United Nations to extend real income comparisons to countries not covered by the full-scale ICP work and to develop annual comparisons for interbenchmark years for the countries covered by the benchmark study. Three approaches will be investigated:

1. Working with data regularly collected by national statistical organizations for their published price indices.
2. Selecting a small sample of prices based on the judgment of experts.
3. Determining analytically (e.g., with multiple regression) the best subset of items that will predict the PPPs at various levels of gross domestic product aggregation.

These data will be collected in a sample of countries and the results will be compared with those produced by the ICP Phase IV benchmark study. Several countries will be directly surveyed by the World Bank. Four Central American countries—Costa Rica, Dominican Republic, Guatemala, and Panama—will be surveyed by consultants in Guatemala. The European Economic Community has agreed to conduct surveys for a group of French-speaking African countries. Data for all these countries will be processed at the World Bank.

The principal products of the project will be a report on reduced information methodology and estimates for the sample of countries, and two reports on the integration of reduced information results with other regional and global estimates.

Responsibility: Economic Analysis and Projections Department—Sultan Ahmad, in collaboration with Professors Irving Kravis, Alan Heston, and Robert Summers of the University of Pennsylvania, and the Centro de Estudios Centroamericanos de Integración y Desarrollo (ECID), Guatemala.

Completion date: June 1982.

Reports

Ahmad, Sultan. "Approaches to Purchasing Power Parity Comparisons Using Shortcuts and Reduced Information." World Bank Staff Working Paper No. 418. September 1980.

———. "Shortcut Methods of International Comparisons of Real Product and Purchasing Power of Currencies." Ph.D. Dissertation, University of Pennsylvania, Philadelphia, 1978.

Agricultural Sector Modeling Conference: A Research Application

Ref. No. 672–24A

The General Algebraic Modeling System (GAMS), now being completed in the Development Research Center, is designed to make mathematical models more generally accessible. The lack of a common documentation system and shared conventions has meant that existing models are difficult to communicate and has been an important barrier to their more widespread use. GAMS uses a language comprehensible to both people and machines, which stays close to the conventions of algebra and is easily transferable among different computers. Because it permits more stages to be automated in the specification and solution of models, the system also reduces the likelihood of errors and makes modeling cheaper and less demanding of highly specialized skills.

GAMS has been used very successfully for the design and operation of models in the area of industrial planning, but it has not yet been applied to models of the agriculture sector. To demonstrate its use in this area, work has begun on the "translation" into GAMS of two models: a model of the agriculture sector in

India, developed by the International Institute for Applied Systems Analysis (IIASA) in Vienna and a model of the agriculture sector in Algeria, developed by the Bureau National d'Etudes du Développement et de l'Economie Rurale (BNEDER) in Algiers, which is collaborating in the project. This work should render the models computationally more accessible and make their structure easier to comprehend. The experience will be documented for presentation at an International Conference on Agriculture Sector Models to be held by IIASA in August 1982.

Responsibility: Eastern Africa Projects Department and Development Research Center—Wilfred V. Candler and Alexander Meeraus, respectively.

Development of a SAM Basis for Planning and Modeling in Egypt

Ref. No. 672-25

The Egyptian economy is going through a period of profound structural change requiring careful economic management. Consequently, a pressing need has been felt for the process of decision making to be based on sound factual grounds. This project is intended to fulfill this need for the Government of the Arab Republic of Egypt both directly and through a collaborative effort with the Development Research and Technical Planning Center (DRTPC) of Cairo University. It aims at strengthening the capacity of the DRTPC to build social accounting matrices (SAMs) and to develop and maintain SAM-based models for development planning.

The major issues facing the Egyptian economy in the 1980s relate to (1) income distribution, (2) pricing policies, (3) inflation, (4) resource mobilization, and (5) investment allocation. The identification of the data and the choice of disaggregations are designed to shed light on these issues. In gathering and organizing the data, one is confronted with the problem that reliable and available information pertains to time periods several years in the past. However, in order to be relevant for policy makers, it is necessary to have access to the most up-to-date data sources. For this reason it is intended that the data would simultaneously be collected for two periods (1977 and 1980/81).

The project is designed in two phases. During the first one, the main focus will be on building the data base and consolidating it in a SAM framework, while the second phase will be concerned with the development of a SAM-based model. The approach followed is to build a set of mutually consistent highly disaggregated accounts and to assemble from them different SAMs, each of which will focus on a particular issue. This would simultaneously achieve the objectives of consistency and flexibility.

Responsibility: Development Research Center—F. Graham Pyatt and Wafik Grais, in collaboration with Boris Pleskovic (consultant), and *Europe, Middle East, and North Africa Programs Department*—Kemal Dervis and Amarendra Bhattacharya, in collaboration with Amir Mohieldin at the Development Research and Technical Planning Center, Cairo University.

Completion date: December 1982.

Reports

Crosswell, M., and Pleskovic, B. "Social Accounting Matrices for Egypt: Outlines and Suggestions for Disaggregation of Individual Accounts." Development Research Center, May 1981.

Multisector and Macroeconomic Models of Structural Adjustment in Yugoslavia

Ref. No. 672-26

This project has two objectives. The first is the construction of a computable general equilibrium (CGE) model of the Yugoslav economy designed to analyze issues of trade and industrial policy and to trace the implications for different sectors of alternative adjustment strategies over the medium term. The second objective is to extend the CGE modeling framework to include variables and phenomena typically handled only by macroeconomic models.

The model being applied to Yugoslavia in the first phase of the project is based on an earlier model of Turkey (see Vinod Dubey, Shakil Faruqi, et al., *Turkey: Policies and Prospects for Growth*, A World Bank Country Study, March 1980, Chapter 7). It will be used as part of a review of Yugoslavia's new Five-Year Plan (1981-85) being carried out by the Europe, Middle East, and North Africa Country Programs Department I. The major new conceptual work in the first phase is the specification of institutional and behavioral relationships appropriate for the Yugoslav economy. When work on its design is completed, the model technology will be transferred to the Europe, Middle East, and North Africa Regional Office for continuing policy work.

CGE models have become increasingly popular because they are able to capture the responses of decentralized decision makers to policy actions that change the structure of incentives in both product and factor markets. At their present state of development, however, they do not adequately treat macroeconomic phenomena, such as inflation, or capture the conflict between policies to influence growth and structural change in the medium term and policies to achieve macroeconomic stabilization in the short term. Macroeconomic models, by contrast, emphasize short-run adjustments and demand management, taking an aggregate view and generally neglecting problems of supply and the structure of production.

The second phase of this project aims to break new ground by incorporating variables, policies, and processes that are common in macroeconomic models into the multisectoral structure of a CGE model. It is intended to explore the theoretical and empirical problems of integrating the two sets of policy concerns within a unified modeling framework. Substantively, the application to Yugoslavia is aimed at improving understanding of both equilibrium and disequilibrium processes at work in a country undergoing structural adjustment to internal and external shocks. Though Yugoslavia's economic institutions are not those of the typical developing country, the underlying economic processes at work and the interactions between macroeconomic and structural variables are fundamentally similar to those characteristics of other semi-industrial countries.

The second phase of the project will be undertaken jointly with a Yugoslav research institute. The goal is to transfer the modeling technology to the research institute so that it can be used for future policy analysis within the country and to draw on the experience and skills of local researchers.

Responsibility: Development Economics Department and Europe, Middle East, and North Africa Country Programs Department I—Sherman Robinson and Suman Bery, respectively, in col-

laboration with Professor Laura Tyson of the University of California, Berkeley.

Completion date: December 1982.

Development of Social Accounts and Models for the Cyprus Five-Year Plan

Ref. No. 672-38

Under this project, the World Bank will collaborate with the Cyprus Planning Bureau in constructing a macroeconomic framework and its associated data base for the Five-Year Development Plan for 1982–86. The project comprises two principal pieces of analysis. First, there is the calculation of detailed and consistent sets of projections for the five-year planning period, under alternative assumptions about external conditions and public policy. To accomplish this, a semi-input-output model will be built. Second, a complete set of shadow prices will be calculated for use in the valuation of public projects and of projects whose undertaking requires some form of consent by government. Particular attention will be paid to the sources of labor in the economy and the ways in which domestic savings and new foreign borrowing might be combined in order to service the considerable foreign debts incurred over the past five years. The model will also be used to examine the effects of changes in taxes and subsidies, in the level and composition of government spending, and in world prices, and the growth of tourism. The estimation of shadow prices requires estimates of how domestic savings and the premium on government income will evolve, a task that will involve the construction of a small, intertemporal optimizing model of growth. Using these estimates, the shadow prices of goods and factors can then be derived from the semi-input-output model.

Responsibility: Europe, Middle East, and North Africa Programs Department II and Development Research Center—Heinz B. Bachman and Clive L. G. Bell, respectively, in collaboration with Shanta Devarajan, Harvard University.

Completion date: June 1982.

The Development and Extension of Macromodeling in Relation to Thailand

Ref. No. 672-47

This project has three interrelated components. The first deals with macroeconomic adjustment in the medium run in Thailand. This component is analyzing past adjustment and recommending further measures to enable the Thai economy to remain on a high growth path without endangering basic macroeconomic equilibrium or creating unacceptable distributional tensions. As the second component, the Bank and the National Economic and Social Development Board (NESDB) of Thailand are constructing a macroeconomic model to provide a common tool of analysis for macroeconomic adjustment issues. The third component will extend the present macroeconomic modeling capacity in two directions: price setting and the appropriate representation of demands for imports, and ways of representing and documenting models to facilitate their implementation and communication.

As it now stands, the model is relatively simple and can be explained as follows. Nominal wage rates and the exchange rate are taken as given, together with the international prices of traded goods other than rice. Within each time period, real investment will also be assumed to be exogenous, as will be land availability and fixed capital in each production activity. Second, the model will assume cost minimizing behavior for each activity and a supply function derived from either a profit or sales maximizing rule. Hence, each activity will have an upward sloping supply curve and commodity markets will be cleared by equalizing demand and supply.

The research will have two phases: in the first phase, an initial version of the new model will be constructed and installed in Bangkok and Washington; in the second phase, improved data will be incorporated in it and further research will be undertaken, including, in particular, experiments with alternative closing rules.

Responsibility: Development Research Center—Wafik M. Grais and Arne Drud; *Economic Analysis and Projections Department*—John D. Shilling and Desmond McCarthy; *East Asia and Pacific Regional Office*—Dusan Vujovic, in collaboration with Phisit Pakkasem, Khun Thamarak Karnpisit, and Piyasawasti

Amranand of the National Economic and Social Development Board of Thailand.

Completion date: July 1983.

Development Paths for Oil Exporters: A Long-Run Macroeconomic Analysis

Ref. No. 672-49

This research project addresses the longer-run development options and problems facing the "capital deficit" oil-exporting economies. Included in this group are: Algeria, Ecuador, Arab Republic of Egypt, Indonesia, Iran, Mexico, Nigeria, Trinidad and Tobago, and Venezuela. Notwithstanding their different structural and institutional features, it is easy to discern a strong central theme of common concern: How to use oil revenues that may be available only for a limited period to promote sustained growth with acceptable distributional characteristics?

The recent experience of industrial, as well as of developing oil exporters, suggests that to use mineral rents productively is not easy, despite the central role played by a rich and diversified natural resource base in the development of a number of economies. With limited linkages between a key rent-producing export sector and the domestic economy, the problem faced by mineral exporters is not unlike that of absorbing large, and possibly volatile, capital inflows. Short-run market signals affected by a rapid increase in absorption out of oil windfalls may provide an indication to producers of investment patterns that are inappropriate to longer-run developmental objectives. The appreciation of real exchange rates, a stagnant agriculture, slow growth of manufacturing, the crowding-out of the private by the public sector, and a trend to dualism are all classic symptoms of the oil economy syndrome, although such effects are not inevitable.

Clearly, the rate at which oil revenues are spent, as well as the spending pattern decided on by government, will influence the extent to which alternative productive sectors are developed and experience is accumulated to assist in raising productivity. Efficient, nonoil tradeable sectors are needed to supplement and eventually replace declining oil revenues as a source of foreign exchange and public revenue. The initial spending decisions, which are essentially political rather than determined by market forces, will also have much impact on income distribution and the extent to which the economy develops along dualistic lines.

Theoretical and empirical analysis of these issues for oil exporters is of relatively recent vintage, although a considerable literature exists on the "export-enclave" economy. Most research in the field of natural resources focuses on the fact that the resources are exhaustibile, rather than on the impact of varying resource rents on the rest of a producing economy. In addition, while analyses of individual producer countries naturally include the role of the oil sector, cross-country analysis has been limited.

The present research project has two components. The objective of the first, comparative, part is to document, analyze, and compare the dynamic options selected by several oil exporters and the consequences for their nonoil economies. As comparators, the experience of developed oil exporters—Norway and the United Kingdom—will also be included. The point of departure in the comparative analysis is a government's decision on how to spend its revenues. Originating from this, multiplier effects, real exchange rate and price changes, and expansion of domestic production capacity affect the evolution of the rest of the economy. The central difficulty—strengthening nonoil tradeable sectors in the face of strong resource pulls towards the construction and service sectors—is common and widely acknowledged in oil-exporting economies concerned about undue dependence on a single, exhaustible source of foreign exchange. Yet, exporting countries have adopted quite divergent development strategies and sectoral priorities. Comparative analysis is an ongoing exercise over the horizon of the project, extending the study undertaken by Alan H. Gelb, listed below. It is planned to include an element of comparative political analysis in this part of the study, which also will draw on the experience of World Bank country economists. A workshop midway through the study is planned to bring together experts from outside the Bank and interested Bank staff.

The second component of the project is to model formally the impact of key policy options for a particular country and to assess the development paths resulting from such choices. In addition to choices involving the selection of extraction rates and total expenditures, sectoral emphasis will need to be addressed. There are some important trade-offs here. If, for example, spending is heavily directed toward infrastructure, domestic inflation is likely, at least for a period, to lead to appreciation of the real exchange rate and the squeezing-out of private manufacturing. An import-intensive investment strategy will place less stress on the domestic economy but reduce the multiplier effects out of oil spending. The analysis will be comparative-dynamic rather than static. Such an exercise will be undertaken for Indonesia, one of the poorest of the oil exporters, and will include the simulation of hypothetical alternative paths over a time frame of twenty to thirty years. Because of the common experience and the broad underlying problems, the modeling exercise will have relevance for other oil exporters. At the same time, the comparative element will prevent research from focusing too exclusively on the special features of one country.

The research will be organized in three stages. In the first stage, a data base will be set up and a preliminary model will be developed. The second stage will cover tuning and simulation of the model. During these stages the comparative analysis will proceed in parallel with the formal modeling. In the third stage, the two components of the research will be completed and written up.

Responsibility: Development Research Center—Alan H. Gelb. A number of consultants will be involved in comparative analysis and data collection.

Completion date: February 1984.

Reports

Gelb, Alan H. "Capital-Importing Oil Exporters: Adjustment Issues and Policy Choice." World Bank Staff Working Paper No. 475. August 1981.

2
International Finance and Trade

Natural Resources and Planning: Issues in Trade and Investment

Ref. No. 671-09

This study is aimed at the formulation and application of commodity models in selected sectors. The ultimate objective of the research is to provide the analytical tools and the data format to analyze global supply and demand conditions of important natural resources and resource-based secondary commodities. The project consists of a number of subprojects focusing on three general topics: investment planning, energy, and the behavior of commodity markets.

A mixed-integer programming model of the copper and bauxite/aluminum industries is used to determine globally optimal investment, production and shipping activities, and regional planning models. In addition to the work directed at formulating investment programs, research on deriving appropriate appraisal rules for projects producing or using nonrenewable natural resources is carried out.

For energy, estimation techniques have been developed that focus on the construction and use of regional energy flow tables relating the flow of energy from primary energy producers through secondary energy producers to final consumers. The model may be used to forecast future energy demands on the basis of price projections.

Research on the dynamics of commodity models focuses attention on issues such as stabilization policies, effects of random shocks on price movements, the nature of extraction costs, and cartelization. Initially, this research involved extending current theoretical frameworks beyond assumptions of constant extraction costs, perfect foresight, and no collusive behavior. Simultaneously, econometric techniques were used to develop several models specific to one or more commodities. The results from these long-run simulations were then used to modify the assumptions (especially on the demand side) underlying the investment planning models. Numerical models along these lines were constructed for jute and copper.

Responsibility: Development Economics Department—Ardy Stoutjesdijk, in collaboration with Hans Bergendorff, Alfredo Dammert, Partha Dasgupta, Geoffrey Heal, E. Hochman, David Kendrick, David Newbery, Robert Pindyck, Joseph Stiglitz, Martin Weitzman, and Pinhas Zusman (consultants).

Completion date: November 1981.

Linkage of Commodity and Country Models

Ref. No. 671-28

Through the construction of a model describing the markets of the main primary commodities, this project aims at providing information on the mechanisms linking the economies of developed and developing countries. This model will make it possible to estimate the impact of business fluctuations in developed countries on prices and the trade of primary commodities. It will also shed light on the factors that affect the foreign exchange earnings of developing countries and on the impact of commodity prices on inflation in developed countries.

The research is done in the context of Project Link, an econometric model of the world economy, which is the result of a cooperative effort by private and official research centers in developed countries, the International Monetary Fund (IMF), the United Nations Centre for Development Planning, Projections and Policies, and the United Nations Conference on Trade and Development (UNCTAD). The Project Link system links together, by trade and price equations, short-run models of the major industrial countries and models of developing regions. The Link model, which is limited to three groups of commodities (food products, fuels, and raw materials), can only give a crude representation of the role of commodity markets in the world economy. This project introduces some 20 commodity models into the Link model, thus improving its relevance to the analysis of development problems and inflation.

Responsibility: Economic Analysis and Projections Department—Peter K. Pollak. Professors L. Klein and F. Gerard Adams of the University of Pennsylvania are directors of the project.

Completion date: November 1981.

Reports

Adams, F. Gerard. "Must High Commodity Prices Depress the World Economy?" *Journal of Policy Modeling* (May 1979).
———. "Primary Commodity Markets in a World Model System." In F.G. Adams and L.R. Klein, *Stabilizing World Commodity Markets.* Lexington, Massachusetts: D.C. Heath, 1978.

Export Incentives in Developing Countries

Ref. No. 671-35

In recent years, several developing countries have expanded their exports of manufactured goods through export incentives. But export incentives have been studied only in general terms and in an aggregated industry format. To provide more useful conclusions, they must be subjected to a more detailed analysis.

The present research project serves this purpose through a cross-section investigation of major export products and a time-series analysis of the effects of export promotion measures. It evaluates, in a comparative framework, the export promotion efforts of three countries (Greece, Republic of Korea, and Pakistan). All the country studies are being carried out with the support of the governments concerned.

Apart from evaluating the export promotion measures used in the three countries under study, this project should yield useful findings for other countries that contemplate the reform of a system of incentives in general and export promotion schemes in particular. It should also aid the World Bank in advising developing countries on export promotion.

The main focus of the country studies is a cross-section investigation of major export products for the latest year for which data are available. Rates of export incentives are estimated and compared with the social profitability of specific exports. Carrying out the investigation at the product level permits consideration of the supply and demand constraints on export expansion, the existence of "cross-subsidization" of exports, and assessment of and reactions to export incentives by individual firms.

The product-by-product analysis will be supplemented by a time-series study of each country's export promotion effort over time and its effect on the growth of exports. Coverage includes traditional as well as nontraditional exports, and agricultural and manufactured goods within each category. Finally, the contribution of export expansion to economic growth is analyzed.

An international synthesis will provide a comparison of the results obtained in each country and for each product. The results will be used to formulate recommendations on the scope and methods of export promotion in developing countries, with emphasis on the countries under study.

Responsibility: Development Research Center—Bela Balassa. Collaborating are the following authors of the country studies: Greece—Demetrious Papageorgiou, Development Economics Department, and Evangelo Voloudakis, Center for Planning and Economic Research, Athens; Korea—Garry Pursell, Industrial Development and Finance Department, Yung W. Rhee, Development Economics Department, and Suk Tai Suh, Korea Development Institute; Pakistan—Mohammed Zubair Khan, Pakistan Development Institute.

Completion date: December 1982.

Reports

The following papers are available from the authors:

Pursell, Garry, and Rhee, Yung W. "A Firm-Level Study of Korean Exports." Research Reports Nos. 1–6 (mimeo):
  No. 1. "Some Institutional Aspects of Incentive Policies."
  No. 2. "Technology."
  No. 3. "Machinery and Equipment, Economies of Scale, and Capacity Utilization."
  No. 4. "Wage and the Demand for Skills."
  No. 5. "Marketing Exports."
  No. 6. "Constraints on Growth in Major Export Markets."
Westphal, Larry E.; Rhee, Yung W.; and Pursell, Garry. "Foreign Factors in Korea's Industrialization." To be published in *Proceedings of the First Annual Conference on Korea Studies:*

The Modernization of Korea and the Impact of the West. Costa
Mesa: University of Southern California, 1980.

"Foreign Influences on Korean Industrial Development." *Oxford
Bulletin of Economics and Statistics* 41 (November 1979)—*Special Issue: The Multinational Corporation.*

Penetration of Industrialized Country Markets by Imports of Manufactures from Developing Countries

Ref. Nos. 671-67 and 671-82

The purpose of these studies is to analyze the effects of increases in imports of manufactured goods from developing countries on product and factor markets in industrial countries (see
also "Research Support for the World Development Report,"
Ref. No. 671-66, in category 1. Development Policy and Planning). The country focus is on Australia, Canada, the European
Economic Community, Japan, Sweden, and the United States.
The studies are examining the extent of import penetration of
markets in the industrial countries by various developing regions
and countries, to determine the market shares of particular
groups of developing countries; determining the impact of competition from developing countries on exports of manufactures of
industrialized countries; and analyzing the factors that lead to
successful protectionist actions against imports from developing
countries, or to high market penetration without such actions.

A major part of the studies consists of the collection and analysis of production and trade data for some 150 product groups.
Various import penetration ratios have been calculated, including
the share of imports in domestic production and consumption,
the rate of change of these import shares, and the growth rate of
consumption for an industry. The economic, social, and political
factors that affect the nature of protection are being analyzed for
each country and for the European Economic Community.

Whether a particular industry obtains protection against
increasing imports seems to depend upon a complex set of economic and political factors relating to that industry. If generalizations of the way these factors operate can be made by analyzing
previous protectionist episodes, the industrial countries could improve their adjustment planning and developing countries could
be helped in planning the industrial composition of the manufac-

tures that are selected for export increases. The studies are, thus, expected to assist both industrial and developing countries in formulating policies that will facilitate a smooth transition for expanded exports of manufactured goods by developing countries and, of course, corresponding export increases by the industrialized countries.

Responsibility: Economic Analysis and Projections Department—Helen Hughes and Vasilis Panoutsopoulos. The principal researchers and institutes associated with the project are Robert Baldwin, University of Wisconsin; Jean Waelbroeck, Free University of Brussels (Belgium), who is coordinating the European Studies, which are taking place at the Overseas Development Institute (United Kingdom); University of Lille (France); Institut für Weltwirtschaft, Kiel (Federal Republic of Germany); Institute for International Economic Studies, Stockholm, and the University of Umea (Sweden); Erasmus University, Rotterdam (Netherlands); Centre for Development Studies, Antwerp (Belgium); and Confederazione Generale dell' Industria Italiana, Canadian North-South Institute, Australian National University, and Japan Economic Research Center.

Completion date: December 1981.

Reports

Anderson, Kym, and Baldwin, Robert E. "The Political Market for Protection in Industrial Countries: Empirical Evidence." World Bank Staff Working Paper No. 492. October 1981.

Bale, Malcolm D., and Mutti, John H. "Output and Employment Changes in a 'Trade Sensitive' Sector: Adjustment in the U.S. Footwear Industry." World Bank Staff Working Paper No. 430. October 1980. Also in *Weltwirtschaftliches Archiv* (June 1981).

Cable, Vincent, and Rebelo, Ivonia. "Britain's Pattern of Specialization in Manufactured Goods with Developing Countries and Trade Protection." World Bank Staff Working Paper No. 425. October 1980.

Evans, John C.; Glenday, Graham; and Jenkins, Glenn P. "Worker Adjustment to Liberalized Trade: Costs and Assistance Policies." World Bank Staff Working Paper No. 426. October 1980.

Glismann, H.H., and Weiss, F.D. "On the Political Economy of Protection in Germany." World Bank Staff Working Paper No. 427. October 1980.

Grilli, Enzo. "Italian Commercial Policies in the 1970s." World Bank Staff Working Paper No. 428. October 1980.

Hamilton, Carl. "Effects of Non-Tariff Barriers to Trade on Prices, Employment and Imports: The Case of the Swedish Textile and Clothing Industry." World Bank Staff Working Paper No. 429. October 1980.

Hughes, Helen, and Waelbroeck, Jean. "Can Developing-Country Exports Keep Growing in the 1980s?" *The World Economy* (June 1981).

Jenkins, Glenn P. "Costs and Consequences of the New Protectionism: The Case of Canada's Clothing Sector." North-South Institute, July 1980.

Koekkoek, K.A.; Kol, J.; and Mennes, L.B.M. "On Protectionism in the Netherlands." World Bank Staff Working Paper No. 493. October 1981.

Lundberg, Lars. "Patterns of Barriers to Trade in Sweden: A Study in the Theory of Protection." World Bank Staff Working Paper No. 494. October 1981.

Tharakan, P.K.M. "The Political Economy of Protection in Belgium." World Bank Staff Working Paper No. 431. October 1980.

Verreydt, Eric, and Waelbroeck, Jean. "European Community Protection against Manufactured Imports from Developing Countries: A Case Study in the Political Economy of Protection." World Bank Staff Working Paper No. 432. October 1980.

Key Institutions and Expansion of Manufactured Exports

Ref. No. 671–68

Exports of manufactured goods from developing countries are growing much faster than their other exports and have become critically important for many of these countries. This project is designed to fill gaps in current knowledge by investigating the practical effects of institutional arrangements in selected areas that are crucial to the exports of manufactured goods, such as nontariff protection and marketing.

Among its objectives, the research seeks to learn more about how to expand manufactured exports and increase their value. A related aim is to gain an increased understanding of the effects of institutionally complex obstacles, such as textile quotas in industrial countries. A third purpose is to learn more about prospects of manufactured exports at the level of particular products and countries. In all these areas, the project builds on previous staff studies and related research, including "Export Incentives in Developing Countries" (Ref. No. 671–35 in this category). The findings are intended to improve the World Bank's advice and its lending operations, while illuminating aspects of manufactured exports that have tended to be neglected in research elsewhere.

A principal focus of this project is research into marketing and related nonprice aspects of exports, by locally owned firms in developing countries, of consumer goods sold in leading industrial countries. This research studies the role in these exports of foreign buyers and intermediaries, such as importers and trading companies, together with the learning processes and expanding operations of the local firm in linking its production to consumer demand overseas. Attention is given, for example, to the shifting division of labor over time between local firms and outside buyers in such areas as contacting wholesalers and retail outlets, choosing designs, organizing delivery, packaging and shipping, and assuring quality control, and to ways in which the unit value of exports can be increased along with their volume. The research also looks at how exports are and can be institutionally promoted at a national level. Interviews for this part of the project have been conducted in Hong Kong, the Republic of Korea, the Philippines, and Thailand, and with firms and institutions involved in this trade in the United States. A study has also been made of the experience in five South American countries— Argentina, Brazil, Colombia, Peru, and Uruguay.

The second focus of the study has been textile quotas against developing countries under the Multifiber Arrangement and their effects on trade in clothing and textiles. Studies have been made of the evolution, functioning, impact, and prospects of this system of managed trade. The system is immensely complex, with several thousand quotas and numerous other details as part of an ever-changing set of agreements restricting the opportunities open to developing countries in exporting clothing and textiles. The potential for exports of these products from low-wage countries is huge and quotas are a major obstacle.

A subsidiary concern is to learn more about the prospects for manufactured exports from developing countries, and find out how to gather better information on their prospects, through interviews with firms and institutions that play key roles in these exports in both developing and developed countries. This part of the study includes discussions with government experts, trade associations, businessmen, and observer analysts in major exporting countries, as well as interviews with major retail and trading companies, multinational firms, public officials, pressure groups, and observer analysts in leading industrial countries.

Responsibility: Development Economics Department—Donald B. Keesing. Recent participants include Martin H. Wolf, Lawrence H. Wortzel, David Morawetz, and Camilo Jaramillo (consultants).

Completion date: December 1982.

Reports

Keesing, D.B., and Wolf, Martin. "Textile Quotas against Developing Countries: A Study of Managed Trade." London: Trade Policy Research Centre, 1980.

————. "Questions in International Trade in Textiles." *The World Economy* 1 (March 1981):79–101.

The Direction of Developing Countries' Trade: Patterns, Trends, and Implications

Ref. No. 672-32

The potential for increased trade among developing countries, the benefits from expanding that potential, the constraints upon it, and the appropriate policy choices have become of increasing interest to analysts and policy makers. This is particularly so in view of a growing belief that prospects for growth and the concomitant expansion of export markets in developed countries are not favorable. Thus, expanded trade among developing countries is seen as a desirable option given the adverse trading environment they face.

This project seeks to analyze some of the underlying issues by examining the characteristics of trade among developing countries and the determinants of the level of their trade in different directions. In the process some light will be shed on such debated questions as:

1. How can countries adjust to shocks in the international environment and take advantage of new trading opportunities?
2. How does the rapid industrialization of some developing countries and the increase in wealth of some mineral and fuel exporters affect the trade of other developing countries?
3. Are there biases against trade among developing countries?
4. Have policies to encourage trade among developing countries had any noticeable effect? Conversely, have policies of import substitution in developing countries been important in thwarting such trade?
5. Is a country's trade regime an important influence on the direction of its trade?
6. Is there a potential for intra-industry trade among developing countries, particularly the more industrially advanced among them?

The research builds upon simpler more descriptive work carried out by Oli Havrylyshyn of George Washington University, in collaboration with Martin Wolf of the Bank's Economic Analysis and Projections Department (EPD). The project will have two distinct phases: The first involves analysis of trade among developing countries using the centralized data bank in EPD; the second will focus on institutional barriers to trade among developing countries such as marketing, credit, and transportation.

The first stage comprises three elements:

1. A "market shares analysis" for five commodity groups of changes in exports by individual developing countries to different destinations.
2. A more detailed examination of the commodity characteristics of the different export baskets, focusing largely on manufactured goods, and using such measures as revealed comparative advantage, weighted average capital-labor ratios of exports in different directions, and indices of intra-industry trade.
3. A "gravity model" analysis, in which the exports of a particular commodity from a country to all country destinations are regressed upon the principal determinants of trade volume: gross domestic product (GDP), GDP per capita, population, and such barriers as transport costs and protection.

The results of the research will help those concerned with

global analysis and policy to assess the potential for, and barriers against, expanded trade among developing countries. For country analysts, the results will assist in the examination of the possibilities for their countries and, more importantly, improve their ability to place their countries' experience in a global context.

Responsibility: Economic Analysis and Projections Department—Martin H. Wolf, in collaboration with Prof. Oli Havrylyshyn of George Washington University (consultant).

Completion date: Phase I—September 1982.

Reports

Havrylyshyn, Oli, and Wolf, Martin H. "Trade Among Developing Countries: Theory, Policy Issues, and Principal Trends." World Bank International Trade and Capital Flows Division Working Paper No. 198–1. February 1981.

Protection and Incentive Systems in the Turkish Manufacturing Sector

Ref. No. 672–36

The objective of this research project is to analyze the system of industrial incentives and the structure of comparative advantage in the Turkish manufacturing sector. This is to be done on the basis of firm-level data and will provide the framework for a comprehensive reform of policies dealing with such issues. The methodology has been developed in an earlier project undertaken in the Development Research Center at the World Bank.[1] It permits the computation from firm-level data of estimates of effective protection, effective subsidy, and domestic resource cost coefficients as well as economic rates of return on capital.

The first stage has been completed with the design of the firm questionnaire and sample, containing 259 firms in 85 manufacturing sectors. The survey is under way. A mission of the World Bank will visit Istanbul in October to transfer the Bank computer program for estimation of indicators of incentives and comparative advantage at the computing facilities of Bosphorus Univer-

---

[1]See Bela Balassa, "Methodology of the West Africa Research Project," mimeo (Development Research Center, February 1977).

sity. The transfer of the computer program will be complemented by trial runs using preliminary firm-level data collected
as part of the project.

The results of the research project will form the basis for a
series of policy papers containing a set of recommendations to
the government and the Bank on the reform of the system of
industrial incentives in Turkey. These recommendations will
cover the system of quantitative import restrictions, the structure
of tariffs, price controls, and export subsidies. They will be implemented in the framework of subsequent structural adjustment
programs undertaken by the Turkish Government with the support of the Bank.

*Responsibility: Europe, Middle East, and North Africa Country
Programs Department II*—Jayanta Roy, Seok Hyun Hong, and
Michel Noel, under the overall advice of Bela Balassa in the De-
velopment Research Center. The research is to be carried out by
a team led by Professor M. Hic of Istanbul University, consisting
of Professor F. Yagci of Bosphorus University, Professor M.
Genceli of Istanbul University, and Professor I. Birdal of Yildaz
Polytechnic Academy.

Completion date: December 1982.

Changes in Comparative Advantage in Manufactured Goods

Ref. No. 672-41

The factors determining international trade in manufactured
goods and the future prospects for this trade are of considerable
interest to country economists, the World Bank's management,
and policy makers in developing countries. The research project
will address itself to these questions by analyzing the pattern of,
and changes in, comparative advantage in manufactured goods
and prospective changes in trade flows.

The first part of the research project represents a major extension and amplification of earlier work by one of the investigators
on the "stages approach" to comparative advantage. The second
part will focus on international specialization in a multilateral
context. Both these parts will involve integrated theoretical propositions and empirical testing.

The paper on "A 'Stages Approach' to Comparative Advantage" by one of the researchers will serve as the point of departure for the first part of the research project.[2] In the course of the research, it is proposed to apply the model to data for a number of years, use time-series data for individual countries, and combine time-series and cross-section data. Bilateral trade relationships will be examined and alternative capital-labor coefficients introduced, with the inclusion of additional factor-intensity and factor-endowment variables. Data on imports as well as on net exports and export-import ratios will be used for alternative formulations of variables representing international specialization. Policy variables will be introduced into the analysis and projections will be made.

The second part of the research project will analyze the determinants of international specialization in a multilateral framework by the use of econometric and simulation methods. The econometric approach to the problem will combine interactions among factor endowments and factor intensities with gravitational elements and demand factors. The employment effects of this trade will further be estimated, and trade flows and employment will be projected by the use of a simulation model.

Responsibility: Development Research Center—Bela Balassa and Roger Bowden.

Completion date: June 1983.

---

[2]Bela Balassa, "A 'Stages Approach' to Comparative Advantage," in Irma Adelman (ed.), *Economic Growth and Resources—Proceedings of the Fifth Congress of the International Economic Association* (Tokyo, Japan: 1977).

3
Agriculture and Rural Development

Analytics of Change in Rural Communities

Ref. No. 671–17

The World Bank has begun to devote substantial amounts of resources to lending for rural development projects. It has become apparent that problems of project design and implementation are more difficult in this area than in more traditional areas of Bank lending. This is due to the fact that (1) the aim of a project often is to initiate or redirect a process of change in rural communities, which raises problems of consistency with the goals of the community itself; and (2) rural development projects involve a variety of activities, some of which do not have any direct short-term economic returns.

The conceptual and information base for the design of rural development projects is still very weak. A great deal of fragmentary knowledge is available about the existing socioeconomic structures of rural communities. But there is relatively little indication of the change these structures would undergo in response to different kinds of intervention, or about the way in which the results from specific village studies can be applied to other villages or regions. The risks of failure are, therefore, greater in rural development projects than in some of the Bank's more traditional investments, and complicated problems of technology, organization, land tenure, and human motivation remain to be resolved.

This project is aimed at building a more comprehensive understanding of the economic structure of rural areas, which would help in the design of policy instruments for rural development. It focuses on a detailed case study of the Muda River Irrigation Project in Malaysia, utilizing the extensive field surveys conducted by the Cooperative Program of the World Bank and the Food and Agriculture Organization (FAO). The study involves the construction of formal models of households' decisions and regional economic activity to assess the effects of the project on incomes and the structure of the local economy. These models encompass: (1) household behavior in respect of production, consumption, and investment decisions; (2) the functioning of local factor markets for land, labor, and capital; and (3) the interactions in the regional economy between agriculture and other economic activities, paying special attention to output, the distribution of income, and final demands. The models also make it possible to identify the points of growth and leakage in the regional economy, and provide a rigorous framework for exploring alternative regional development strategies.

Responsibility: Development Research Center—Clive L.G. Bell.

Completion date: March 1982.

Reports

Bell, Clive L.G. "The Future of Rice Monocultures in Malaysia." In Priscilla Reining and Barbara Lenkerd (eds.), *Village Viability in the Contemporary World*, Proceedings Volume of the Conference of the American Association for the Advancement of Science, February 1978. Boulder, Colorado: Westview Press, 1980.

Bell, Clive L.G., and Devarajan, Shanta. "Semi-Input-Output and Shadow Prices: A Critical Note." *Oxford Bulletin of Economics and Statistics* 42 (August 1980).

_____. "Towards a Synthesis of Semi-Input-Output and Little-Mirrlees: A Social Cost-Benefit Analysis with Multiplier Effects of an Irrigation Project in Northwest Malaysia." *Pakistan Development Review* 18 (September 1979).

Bell, Clive L.G., and Hazell, Peter B.R. "Measuring the Indirect Effects of an Agricultural Investment Project on its Surrounding Region." *American Journal of Agricultural Economics* 62 (February 1980).

Hazell, Peter B.R. "Endogenous Input Prices in Linear Programming Models." *American Journal of Agricultural Economics* 61 (August 1979).

Programming and Designing Investment:
Indus Basin

Ref. No. 671–45

Formulation of agriculture and irrigation projects often depends on implicit policy assumptions and on complex technical relationships that are rarely explored at the appraisal stage. The principal objectives of this research are (1) to test the meaningful integration of complex physical relationships between surface and groundwater into an economic planning model; (2) to test the sensitivity of project design to the inclusion of objectives other than economic efficiency; and (3) to construct an investment planning model for the Indus Basin in Pakistan that will quantify the trade-offs between multiple welfare objectives in investment project design and agricultural development policy.

Static linear programming is employed to characterize the Indus Basin, using an objective function that simulates producer response to policy intervention. The data base for the estimation of model parameters comes principally from a parallel study carried out by the Water and Power Development Authority (WAPDA) of the Government of Pakistan and funded in part by a United Nations Development Programme (UNDP) project, for which the World Bank was Executing Agent.

The basin-level model includes component models that are integrated via a module representing the network of canals, reservoirs, and other basin-level constraints. The component models in turn characterize the agricultural production and the hydrology of the fresh and saline water aquifers of 53 different regions of the basin. Each of these component models includes a farm-level model to simulate producer response to changes in resource endowment due to public investment. The farm-level models have a modular construction to facilitate efficient design of the many models of this type, including specialization of crop and livestock activities for nine different agroclimatic zones of the basin.

Thus, the basin-level model will simulate the integrated use of groundwater and surface water throughout the Indus Basin. While the inclusion of groundwater greatly complicates the model structure, it is necessary if the relevant set of investment projects is to be modeled in a meaningful way. Moreover, given significant basin-level interdependence on a crucial input—water—that is neither marketed nor priced in any realistic sense, project design and appraisal are quite sensitive to the specification of the institutional arrangements for the allocation of water.

Another set of simulation experiments will allow a rigorous consistency test of the hypotheses underlying planned water-related investments. In these and other experiments, the effects of alternative policies will be examined via parametric programming. A range of simulations will be made to assess the efficacy of alternative investment programs and policy instruments in meeting various goals. The mode of analysis is comparative-static in order to be able to include sufficient microeconomic detail to facilitate project design and appraisal. Technical change and some other dynamic elements, however, can be analyzed by solving the model with parameter estimates that represent various points in time.

Arrangements have been made for the recasting of several components of the model family for operational use by the Planning Division of the Water and Power Development Authority of Pakistan and their transfer to Pakistan. This will entail training of WAPDA technical personnel by members of the Development Research Center.

Responsibility: Development Research Center—John H. Duloy and Gerald T. O'Mara, in collaboration with the South Asia Regional Office and the Water and Power Development Authority of Pakistan.

Completion date: December 1981.

Reports

Bisschop, J.; Candler, W.; Duloy, J.H.; and O'Mara, G.T. "The Indus Basin Model: A Special Application of Two-Level Linear Programming." In *Mathematical Programming* (forthcoming).

Distribution of Income through the Extended Family System

Ref. No. 671–57

In the World Bank's strategy to assist the development of the Sahel, irrigation plays an increasingly important role as a means to expand useful employment and to reduce the risk of crop failures and famine. In this endeavor, the Bank almost completely lacks information about three important aspects of introducing modern irrigation projects within the context of the traditional African extended family system:

1. To whom do the incremental revenues created by irrigation projects accrue?
2. How does irrigation fit into or upset the traditional pattern of task allocation among family members?
3. To what extent are changes in traditional societies explained by (a) the increasing use of cash, (b) the sale of farm crops to an outside market, or (c) the need to adapt to orders from outside about methods of cultivating irrigated crops?

Knowledge of these elements is important for the design and organization of projects as well as for their justification. Work bottlenecks vary considerably according to the number of persons working on each plot, as does the need for mechanization. For project justification, it is important to know more about the number of beneficiaries and their economic and social status, particularly for the Sahel, where irrigation projects tend to be rather expensive.

The results expected from the study will have operational significance for the design of irrigation projects in Senegal, Mauritania, and possibly Mali, and may be relevant for irrigation projects in other river basins in the Sahel with sociological conditions and problems similar to those in the Senegal Valley. Also, the design and methodology of the study, as well as the insights gained from its implementation, may have wider applicability.

Four different societies (Wolof, Toucouleur, Soninké, and a modern settler society) live along the Senegal side of the river from St. Louis to Bakel. Distinct in language and in the complexity of their social systems, these societies are similar in that the largest unit of settlement is the village, which serves to distribute different amounts of revenue to different individuals. Each of these villages grows its own food in three different ways (rainfed agriculture, flood recession irrigation, animal husbandry) with a fourth, modern, type of irrigation cultivation now being added. Every person able to walk works at this subsistence type of agriculture. Consequently, participation in a work team is essential in order to obtain a share of the harvest.

Ethnographic descriptions of single villages and descriptive statistics available from official organizations reveal the possible units of production that may be selected for study: (1) the extended family compound (gallé); (2) the unit within that compound that eats together (feu); (3) the unit, within that compound, that sleeps in the same set of rooms (ménage). This seems to remain true under the new methods of irrigation.

The system, as described above, is deduced from the literature and some observation, and as such is no more than a working hypothesis. The aim of this study is to test the hypothesis through careful analysis of all existing information plus additional field work. In 10 villages, some 150 households were visited twice: the first time, in September 1977, to cover the year 1976 and the second time, in December of the same year, to cover 1977. The study examines specifically how the proceeds are apportioned among such obligations as rent, sharecropping, and shares that go by custom to other members of the extended family, or to religious authorities.

The bulk of the field work and part of the data preparation and analysis were carried out by the Société Nationale des Etudes de Développement (SONED), a consultant firm established by the Senegalese Planning Ministry. In addition, a sociological and economic study group within the Société d'Aménagement et d'Exploitation des Terres du Delta (the public company in charge of developing irrigation along the Senegalese side of the valley) closely follows the study and shares in the experience gained by its implementation.

Responsibility: Western Africa Regional Office—Heinz B. Bachmann and Jan Weijenberg. The bulk of the research was undertaken by Professor John Mogey of Boston University, in collaboration with SONED and with Abdel Majid Slama of the Centre National des Etudes Agricoles, Tunis, as agricultural economist.

Completion date: A draft report was completed in September 1981 and is available from Heinz B. Bachmann. A revised draft is scheduled for distribution in September 1982.

Evaluation of Food Distribution Schemes

Ref. No. 671-80

This study is part of the Food Security Work Program within

the Agriculture and Rural Development Department of the World Bank and follows up on a previous research project, "Projections of the Extent of Food Deficits of Target Groups under Alternative Policy Programs" (Ref. No. 671–64), now completed. In the earlier project, a methodology was developed to relate the caloric intake of different groups to income and food price levels and to project the state of malnutrition under policy alternatives. This methodology was applied in eight country case studies. It demonstrated the extent to which malnutrition is a widespread and serious problem in developing countries and suggested that, in many of them, food distribution and intervention schemes will continue to be necessary.

Currently, information on the effectiveness of food distribution and intervention schemes is lacking. Further, no satisfactory method exists for (1) estimating the required scale of food distribution systems; (2) projecting their costs and benefits under alternative development strategies; and (3) evaluating the costs and benefits of basic needs programs in rural development projects. The primary objective of this research project is to study the operational aspects of food distribution systems and explore alternative approaches to evaluating their effectiveness.

This study has several parts:

1. A survey evaluating current food distribution systems and how they operate.
2. An empirical study of alternative food distribution systems, their impact on several variables and associated fiscal costs, and on economic costs and benefits.
3. The exploration of alternative methodologies for the evaluation of food distribution systems and basic needs programs.

Some of the results expected from this research are:

1. An assessment of the operational problems associated with alternative food distribution and intervention schemes.
2. Estimates of fiscal costs, losses in producer incomes, consumption by subsistence producers, and leakages to unintended beneficiaries of food distribution schemes.
3. A methodology and program for evaluating alternative food distribution systems.
4. An assessment of alternative methodologies to evaluate basic needs programs in nutrition.
5. Estimates of the social demand function for basic food needs.

Responsibility: Agriculture and Rural Development Department—Pasquale L. Scandizzo, in collaboration with Odin K. Knudsen, South Asia Projects Department, and Gurushri N. Swamy, Economic Analysis and Projections Department.

Completion date: December 1982.

Reports

Harbert, L., and Scandizzo, Pasquale L. "Food Distribution and Nutrition Intervention: The Case of Chile." World Bank Staff Working Paper (forthcoming).

Knudsen, O. "Economics of Supplemental Feeding of Malnourished Children: A Case of Leakages, Benefits and Costs." World Bank Staff Working Paper No. 451. April 1981.

———. "Nutrition and Food Needs—South Asia, A Review of Research on Magnitudes, Policy and Prospects." Working Paper presented at IFT Annual Meeting, Atlanta, Georgia, June 1981.

Knudsen, O., and Scandizzo, Pasquale L. "The Demand for Calories in Developing Countries." Agricultural Research and Economic Policy Division Working Paper No. 26. October 1980.

———. "Price Policy and Basic Needs: Implications and Estimates." Agricultural Research and Economic Policy Division Working Paper No. 41. April 1981.

Scandizzo, Pasquale L., and Graves, J. "The Alleviation of Malnutrition: Impact and Cost Effectiveness of Official Programs." Agricultural Research and Economic Policy Division Working Paper No. 19. March 1979.

Scandizzo, Pasquale L., and Knudsen, Odin K. "The Evaluation of the Benefits of Basic Needs Policies." In *American Journal of Agricultural Economics* 62 (February 1980):46–57. Also World Bank Reprint Series: Number 138.

Scandizzo, Pasquale L., and Swamy, Gurushri. "Benefits and Costs of Food Distribution Policies: The India Case." World Bank Staff Working Paper (forthcoming).

Swamy, Gurushri. "Public Food Distribution in India." Agricultural Research and Economic Policy Division Working Paper No. 25. July 1979.

India: Impact of Agricultural Development on Employment and Poverty (Phase II)

Ref. No. 671-89

The objective of Phase II of this research (Phase I, Ref. No. 671-62, has now been completed) is to produce a better understanding of some of the policy and investment alternatives for alleviating poverty in rural India, by studying their effects in a number of specific institutional, infrastructural, and agroclimatic contexts. In particular, policies such as investment in irrigation works (public and private), increased availability of credit through public lending institutions, and expansion of nonfarm employment opportunities will be the focal points of the research. In studying these policies' effects, it is assumed that the preexisting institutions and infrastructures are extremely important. To capture their variations, the research will concentrate on three areas: Andhra Pradesh, Punjab, and Bihar. Punjab, at one extreme, represents a dynamic agriculture, based on the availability of irrigation (private and public), increasing mechanization, and "capitalistic" modes of production. Certain areas of Bihar represent almost a polar opposite of semifeudal stagnant agriculture. Andhra Pradesh falls between the two.

The second major initial assumption is that the impact on rural households of public policy is filtered and possibly distorted through the prism of an interlocked set of transactions between households. In the absence of a complete set of smoothly functioning markets for inputs and outputs, rural households enter into simultaneous transactions in more than one commodity or service with each other. This linking could also reflect the distribution of economic-political power among households. As the effects of public policy interventions in this system may be completely frustrated or be the opposite of their ostensible objectives, it is proposed to study these interlinkages in some detail.

While institutional changes cannot be ruled out, at least in principle, given the past history of implementation of land reform and tenancy laws, the important question is: How far can agricultural development be pushed through public policy with a favorable impact on poverty, without major institutional change? The proposed research addresses this question.

Phase I set out a tentative methodology and identified the data requirements. As the preexisting data were inadequate to test the methodology, primary data collection is one of the major tasks of Phase II.

Responsibility: Development Research Center—Clive L.G. Bell and Chalongphob Sussangkarn, in collaboration with T.N. Srinivasan (consultant), the Indian Institute of Management, Ahmedabad, and the Agro-Economic Research Center, Waltair.

Completion date: June 1984.

Reports

Bell, C., and Zusman, P. "Towards a General Bargaining Theory of Equilibrium Sets of Contracts—The Case of Agricultural Rental Contracts." Presented at the World Congress of the Econometric Society, Aix-en-Provence, France, August–September 1980.

Braverman, A., and Srinivasan, T.N. "Interrelated Credit and Tenancy Markets in Rural Economies of Developing Countries." Development Research Center Discussion Paper No. 30 August 1979. Also in the *Journal of Development Economics* (forthcoming).

Braverman, A., and Stiglitz, J.E. "Landlords, Tenants and Technological Innovations." Mimeo. World Bank, April 1981.

————. "Sharecropping and the Interlinking of Agrarian Markets." Mimeo. World Bank, May 1981.

China's Rural Development Experience

Ref. No. 671-90

Over the past thirty years, China has accumulated valuable experience in the sphere of agricultural development. The government has effectively organized a nation of 950 million people, 80 percent of whom live in the rural sector, and has successfully tackled a number of major development problems:

- The rural labor force has been mobilized to work on large-scale public works projects.
- The difficulties encountered in disseminating agricultural technology have been reduced through the creation of an efficient extension service.
- Production and distribution policies have largely eliminated malnutrition among the populace.

- The development of human resources has been accelerated by innovative health care programs and heavy investment in schooling.

The primary objective of this research will be to synthesize the available material on rural development in China and to develop a conceptual framework for subsequent comparative analyses. The study will enlarge the Bank's understanding of the rural economy in China and help to integrate the Chinese developmental experience with that of other major developing nations.

The study will be divided into three parts. The first part will deal with trends in agricultural production, combined with an evaluation of the essential input-output relations within the rural economy. Particular attention will be paid to the efficiency and impact of rural industrialization. In the second part, the welfare of the rural populace will be analyzed. Such issues as the distribution of income, the provision of medical services, rural education, and nutritional requirements will be covered.

The final part will be concerned with the political and organizational aspects of rural development. The organizational skills of the Chinese government have made possible the mobilization of the country's human resources for the purposes of economic advancement, but the creation and maintenance of this massive organizational system has brought many problems in its wake. China has tackled these problems in a highly innovative fashion, which is instructive for development experts faced with similar difficulties elsewhere. Furthermore, an analysis of organizational change in China provides valuable clues as to the future productive potential of the Chinese economy and its stability.

Responsibility: Policy Planning and Program Review Department—Shahid Yusuf and S. J. Burki, in collaboration with Dwight Perkins of Harvard University (consultant).

Completion date: The final report has been completed.

The Construction of Econometric Models for the Supply of Perennials: A Case Study of Natural Rubber and Tea in Sri Lanka

Ref. No. 672-02

The "tree crop problem," i.e., the development of well-specified structural econometric models for the supply of peren-

nial crops, has long defied a satisfactory solution. In view of the
heavy reliance of many developing countries on perennial crops
to provide necessary foreign exchange earnings, this is an issue of
considerable importance to the World Bank. Replanting and re-
habilitation projects for perennials have historically accounted for
a significant proportion of the Bank's agricultural investment
portfolio. But the fact that demand and short-run supply functions are both inelastic with respect to price has caused great in-
stability in world prices of perennial crops, and hence in the export earnings of producers. Balancing the need of governments to
extract sufficient surplus from the export of cash crops (through
the imposition of export duties) against the need of farmers for
sufficient profits to warrant new planting and replanting with improved clonal varieties and intensive use of fertilizers has proved
to be an extremely difficult problem. Despite the plethora of subsidies and other incentives, such policies have rarely succeeded in
stimulating the smallholder. As a result, in many developing
countries the existing stock of perennials is not only overaged,
but also contains an excessive proportion of low-yielding clonal
material.

   One of the important obstacles to a thorough examination of
the tree-crop problem has been the lack of systematic data on the
age structure and clonal composition of existing stands. Unfortunately, in many of the developing countries the available data on
perennials consist only of macro time series on output, producer
prices, area under cultivation, and the array of government incentives and taxes. In some cases, data on wages and labor inputs, on
new plantings and replantings, inputs and prices of materials (notably fertilizer), and on climatic conditions are also available. As
a result of differences and gaps in the data base, researchers have
been forced to specify overly simple models which fail to capture
many of the important features of the problem. The inability to
incorporate age structure and clonal mix in the form of a vintage
model of perennial production has substantially hampered a
quantitative assessment of the effects of alternative government
tax and incentive schemes on replanting, new plantings, the use
of inputs, and the trajectory of future output.

   The objective of this pilot project is to explore the feasibility
of constructing vintage models of perennial supply via a case
study of the rubber and tea sectors in Sri Lanka. For both sectors, extensive published macro time-series data exist, covering

upwards of forty years. In the case of rubber, these include age structure and (since 1953) clonal mix. Various surveys, within the last 10 years, of smallholders and estates in the two sectors will supplement the aggregate data. The Government of Sri Lanka has provided access to previously unpublished data obtained from individual rubber estate records covering the past 10 years.

The Bank has collaborated with the two state plantation corporations to extract data for a sample of fifty rubber estates from annual accounting statements and field record books. These records, not previously assembled in usable form, provide a wealth of detailed information on age distribution, clonal mix, labor inputs and wages, expenditures on other factors of production, fertilizer usage, and tapping systems and intensities. The data make it possible to develop vintage models of rubber and tea production applicable at micro and macro levels. Thus, the first phase of the project involved collaboration with the Central Bank of Ceylon to collect and organize aggregate and estate level data on rubber and tea from both published and unpublished sources.

As presently envisaged, the models will address the new planting and replanting decisions of estates and smallholders and their relation to producer prices, government subsidy payments, and anticipated yields; the relationship of yields to age structure, clonal mix, labor, other inputs, and climatic conditions; the depletion of existing stands over time; the use of inputs in relation to input and producer prices; tapping intensities and plucking rounds and their relation to wage rates, prices, climatic conditions, and elevation; and the effect of changes in the price structure of grades of processed output on the output mix. The models will also incorporate such policy variables as export duties, export cesses, subsidies for replanting, the use of fertilizer, and varieties of planting materials. Hence, they should permit a systematic evaluation of the consequences of alternative incentive schemes on usage of inputs, the output of crops, associated foreign exchange earnings, and the flow of government revenues for other purposes. It is hoped that the research will be of use to government planners in Sri Lanka.

To assess whether models such as these could be used in countries that do not have as complete a data base, a series of experiments will be conducted. Increasingly more complex models will be specified, estimated, and tested, in order to pinpoint the deficiencies and sources of bias in the parameter estimates and resulting projections. These experiments should provide valuable guidelines as to which are the most useful models (given the constraints of available data) and should also help in establishing priorities for the use of resources in collecting more comprehensive data in other countries.

It is expected that the project will result in a series of research papers and possibly a monograph.

Responsibility: Development Economics Department—Michael J. Hartley, with the collaboration of R. Kyle Peters, Jr. (researcher). Professor Marc Nerlove, Northwestern University, and Professor Dan Etherington, Australian National University, are consultants.

Collaboration with the Government of Sri Lanka in the collection and organization of data and the administration of the rubber estate questionnaire is being coordinated by the Statistics Department of the Central Bank of Ceylon under the overall supervision of Dr. K.S.E. Jayatillake, Director of Statistics; primary responsibility for the estate questionnaire will be borne by M.D.D. Gunatillake, Assistant Director of Statistics; Sunil Fernando, Senior Assistant Director and Chief of the Economic Indicators Division, is responsible for the collection of the macro data. Extraction of data from historical records at each of the estates has been organized by the two state corporations—the Sri Lanka State Plantations Corporation and the Janatha Estates Development Board.

Completion date: June 1982.

Land Tenure and Labor Markets in Indonesia

Ref. No. 672-08

Little is known about how land tenure arrangements in Java have changed over time, and how they affect access to employment and living standards in rural areas. Earlier small-scale studies in Indonesia put forward several propositions that will be more rigorously tested in the present study. For example, the Land Reform Act of 1960 conferred individual property rights where village land had previously been communally controlled. This appears to have made it easier for farmers to sell land and to have unintentionally encouraged the concentration of ownership, with adverse effects on the welfare of poorer groups.

This study will examine whether concentration of landownership has been increasing in lowland rice villages in Java, where at present 10 percent to 20 percent of the villagers own 60 percent to 80 percent of the agricultural land, while about half the villagers own none. Only about one-fifth of the householders in these villages own enough land to produce all their own food; the other 80 percent are landless or marginal farmers. As landownership becomes more concentrated and absentee ownership increases, the traditional mechanisms of support for the poor are being destroyed. As a result of these trends, it is feared that the lowland population may become increasingly vulnerable to food shortages in times of severe drought.

Based on the analysis of existing micro-level survey data, the research aims at identifying the factors that result in landlessness, the sale of land to outsiders, and concentration of ownership. Part of the investigation will review changes, over the past eighty years, in landownership, landlessness, and concentration of land control, and assess the role played by land taxation. The project will also examine the commercialization of land, analyze the institutional changes occurring in renting and sharecropping, and assess the impact of growing concentration of landownership on the welfare of villagers.

Responsibility: World Bank Resident Mission in Indonesia— Bhanoji Rao, with the collaboration of Rudolf Sinaga (Director, Rural Dynamics Study) and William Collier as advisors. The research will be undertaken primarily by the Rural Dynamics Study (RDS), a research component of the Agro Economic Survey at Bogor, East Java, which is an interministerial research organization for the formulation and evaluation of government policy on the agricultural economy of Indonesia.

Completion date: December 1981.

A Framework for Agriculture Sector Analysis

Ref. No. 672-11

This project aims at improving the methods available for agriculture sector analysis. It will adapt and combine several techniques developed for economywide planning into a single framework. By permitting three levels of aggregation to be handled together—the subsector (particular commodities, investment programs, or project areas, for example), the agriculture sector as a whole, and the national economy—the framework should make it easier to trace links among sectors and gauge the interactions between the consequences of decisions at the sectoral level and at the project level. The approach should be more convenient for short-term and medium-term planning than the present generation of linear programming models.

The framework is being designed to be applicable in various degrees of sophistication, depending on the amount of data, manpower, finance, and time available to the analyst. It starts from three conceptual approaches that are progressively more complex: the material balance technique, based on commodity accounting; semi-input-output analysis; and the social accounting matrix.

The full framework will have two essential aspects: descriptive, based on an accounting system detailing the flows of income and expenditure among the main participants in the agricultural economy; and interpretative, based on an input-output framework establishing technical and institutional relations among incomes, expenditures, and commodity flows. Even in its simplest form—commodity accounting—the framework can be used to interpret the agricultural economy and to link investment decisions from the level of the commodity, or subsectors, to the level of the sector and the economy as a whole. Using a semi-input-output analysis (SIO) mathematical programming model (MP) and a social accounting matrix (SAM), the framework is capable of evaluating larger projects, or groups of projects, taking into account both their direct and indirect effects throughout the economy.

The SIO-MP-SAM models are being developed, estimated, and tested for the agriculture sector of Portugal and Fiji. The Portuguese set of models is being used to study medium-term needs for public investment and the effects of progressive application of the common agricultural policy of the European Economic Community. Collaborating institutions in Portugal are the Gulbenkian Foundation of Agricultural Economics, the Basic Study Group on the Industrial Economy of the Ministry of Industry and Technology, and the Financial Institute of Agriculture and Fisheries Development. Work on data collection, model formulation, and testing has already been completed and a full set of preliminary results is available. The results conform to the hypothesis that modeling can begin from a single commodity balance approach and, then, more dimensions of accounting can be added to this nucleus.

In the Fiji case, the project is still at the stage of data collection. Once this is completed the models will be used to analyze the income distribution and implications of resource use of alternative development programs, especially those that relate to the transformation of subsistence agriculture and the balance between the agriculture sector and the rest of the economy.

Responsibility: Agriculture and Rural Development Department—Pasquale L. Scandizzo and Graham F. Donaldson.

Completion date: June 1982.

Agricultural Innovations in India: A District and Farm Level Analysis of Fertilizer Use and HYV Adoption

Ref. No. 672-14

While similar to previous decades in aggregate terms, the growth of agricultural output in India over the last ten to fifteen years has been qualitatively different in that it has resulted largely from increases in yield rather than increases in cropped area. The increasingly intensive use of "modern" inputs like fertilizers and high yielding varieties (HYV) of seeds has been mainly responsible for the improvement in yields. This study proposes to examine in depth the factors influencing the adoption of these "new" inputs by farmers in various parts of India.

An analysis of the determinants of the adoption of these innovations will provide answers to a range of policy-related questions. What has determined the spread of these innovations? Has nonadoption of these inputs been a function of a lack of knowledge or nonprofitability of inputs for particular farm conditions? What role have relative prices played in the adoption process? What has been the contribution of extension services to farm productivity? Thus, a major objective of this research is to assess the role that various factors—farmer characteristics (e.g., education), farm characteristics (e.g., soil quality, irrigation), and policy variables such as fertilizer prices, output prices, and the provision of extension services—have played in the process of adoption. Knowledge of the economic forces determining adoption, will be useful in shaping policies aimed at increasing farm production.

Answers to the above questions will be sought through analysis of household and district level data for the years 1970-71, 1975-76, and 1976-77. The behavior of farmers growing the two major crops—wheat and rice—will be specifically examined. Analysis both at the household and district level will be conducted because the results from these analyses are complementary to an understanding of the process of adoption. Household level analysis can indicate the role of factors determining adoption at a point in time. District level data for two different time periods (e.g., 1970-71 and 1976-77) can be used to evaluate factors determining the speed with which the new practices are adopted.

Responsibility: Development Economics Department—Surjit S. Bhalla, in collaboration with Prannoy L. Roy and Pulin Nayak of the Delhi School of Economics, Delhi University, India.

Completion date: June 1983.

Improved Technology for Animal-Powered Agriculture

Ref. No. 672-17

This research project is examining the "state of the art" with respect to the equipment complex based on animal draft power and will seek to identify the determinants of observed equipment changes in selected farming situations. Within these two broad objectives, the project is intended to provide general insights and information about animal-powered farming for support of project proposals and policy recommendations, and to improve understanding of the economics of animal-powered farming within the context of a given country.

Because the introduction of animal power in agriculture must take into account whether the technical innovations are suitable for the farmers, and whether the farmers will accept the equipment, the study will (1) review the existing "shelf" of improved forms of implements; (2) examine the incentives to which innovative farmers have responded and the constraints to which both they and the suppliers of improved implements have adjusted;

and (3) assess the costs and benefits of these developments to individuals and society.

Responsibility: Agriculture and Rural Development Department—Graham F. Donaldson, in collaboration with the staff of the World Bank Resident Mission, New Delhi.

Completion date: Phase I—October 1981.

Food Policy Analysis for Practitioners

Ref. No. 672-18

The objective of the project is to examine, reconcile, and incorporate production and consumption issues in the process of formulating food policies in developing countries.

The work plan for the project consists of the following steps: (1) a review of the literature on food and nutrition planning; (2) a review of a few recent studies that are particularly relevant for food planning, even though they are directed at the broader issue of policies for agricultural development; (3) a new synthesis of analytical work in other related agricultural fields, putting it into an operational context; (4) an analysis of the conceptual framework of food policies; and (5) a critical appraisal of practical approaches to preparing strategies for food development.

Responsibility: Agriculture and Rural Development Department—Graham F. Donaldson, in collaboration with Professors W. Falcon and S. Pearson of the Stanford Food Research Institute and Professor P. Timmer of Harvard University.

Completion date: December 1981.

The Impact of Agricultural Extension: A Case Study of the Training and Visit Method in Haryana, India

Ref. No. 672-29

Agricultural extension is widely perceived as an important mechanism for transmitting the results of agronomic research to farmers, thus helping them to increase the productivity of the land and water at their disposal. At the same time, the feedback from farmers through the extension system can be used to ensure that agricultural research concentrates on farmers' needs.

One particular kind of extension organization, the Training and Visit (T&V) system, has been adopted in many of the Bank's member countries, as it seems to be more effective than other systems in improving farmers' performance. The essence of this system is a tightly structured work program for agents, based on a strict schedule of visits to groups of farmers, each of which includes selected contact farmers; training and updating sessions for agents; a hierarchical organizational structure, with clearly defined duties and responsibilities; and exclusive devotion to extension work. At the initial stage, the T&V extension method stresses improved practices that are likely to require additional labor rather than the increased use of costly material inputs, in the expectation that small farmers with surplus family labor will find such innovations easier to adopt. More complex changes are recommended at later stages.

After its introduction in Turkey in the late 1960s, the T&V system is being implemented in many countries. Preliminary data collected by monitoring and evaluation units in these projects suggest that yields have grown significantly, a large proportion of farmers have adopted the recommended practices, and the increases in yields are positively related to the number of improved practices adopted.

These findings are not conclusive, however. There is a clear need for a detailed study of (1) the extent to which extension agents cause, or hasten, farmers' adoption of recommended practices; (2) the extent to which recommended practices are adopted at different rates by different classes of farmers; (3) factors that enhance or retard farmers' adoption; and (4) the effects of the extension system on farm productivity.

This research project will address the issues raised above, by undertaking a two-year case study of the agricultural extension system in the State of Haryana, India, which was reorganized as a T&V system in 1979. The study will use survey data to be collected over four consecutive crop seasons. Standard statistical analysis will be used as well as more advanced econometric methods, such as Probit-type discrete choice models. With these tools, the study will evaluate, in quantitative terms and for different classes of farmers, the effects of the extension system and other variables on farmers' adoption of better agricultural practices, and the effects of these changes in behavior on the use of material inputs (such as fertilizer and seeds), cropping patterns, and yields.

The results will add to the understanding of how farmers adopt new technologies and the role that extension can play in increasing farm productivity. Since the research will include the detailed specification of variables describing the coverage, intensity, and focus of extension contacts (such as the frequency of contacts per season, the number of farmers covered by an agent, or the size and composition of the group of contact farmers), it will be possible to draw inferences about the effects of changes in the design of the extension service. The study will also help to improve the techniques used for monitoring and evaluating agricultural extension projects.

Responsibility: Development Research Center and *South Asia Programs Department*—Gershon Feder and Roger H. Slade, respectively, in collaboration with Haryana Agricultural University, Hissar.

Completion date: January 1984.

Reports

Feder, G. "Adoption of Interrelated Agricultural Innovations: Complementarity and the Impacts of Risk, Scale and Credit." Development Research Center Working Paper. May 1981. Also in *American Journal of Agricultural Economics* (forthcoming, February 1982).

Feder, G.; Just, R.; and Zilbermann, D. "Adoption of Agricultural Innovations in Developing Countries: A Survey." World Bank Staff Working Paper No. 444. February 1981.

Feder, G., and O'Mara, G.T. "On Information and Innovation Diffusion: A Bayesian Approach." Development Research Center Working Paper. May 1981. Also in the *American Journal of Agricultural Economics* (forthcoming, February 1982).

Feder, G., and Slade, R. "The Monitoring and Evaluation of Training and Visit Extension in India: A Manual of Instruction." Mimeo. World Bank, August 1981.

Production and Distributional Implications of Dairy Development Projects: Effects on Incomes, Consumption, and Nutrition of the Poor

Ref. No. 672-30

The targeting of benefits towards the poor has played an increasing role in the World Bank's choice and design of agricultural and rural development projects. Techniques such as social cost-benefit analysis have been used to integrate distributional effects into project design. However, techniques for measuring the distribution of benefits from these projects, and their actual effects on the poor, are limited, and this has hampered the design of new projects. Specifically, not much is known about how projects affect:

- household food consumption and nutritional status;
- farm investment, and through investment, future production;
- incomes and institutions through the multiplier effects of increased production;
- the incomes and consumption of poor households that are not among the projects' direct beneficiaries, as a result of project-induced changes in relative prices and employment.

This study attempts to remedy these deficiencies for dairy development projects by looking at the actual effects on (1) production and labor allocation, (2) income distribution, and (3) human nutrition of the Rajasthan and Karnataka Dairy Development Projects in India. The study will:

1. Estimate the direct economic benefits produced by the projects.
2. Estimate how project benefits are being distributed, paying particular attention to the projects' impact on the incomes of the poor.
3. Estimate how the projects are affecting food consumption (including food distribution within a family) and nutrition among the poor and population groups that are deficient in calories and protein.
4. Identify and quantify the key relationships and parameters determining the effects of a project on production, food consumption, and nutrition.
5. Develop a system for evaluating the economic and nutritional effects of dairy development projects.

Data will be gathered through household surveys. In the Karnataka study, a primarily cross-sectional survey will be undertaken whereby households that have participated in the project for from one to four years, as well as households not yet participating, will be sampled. This sample of approximately 1,000 households will be surveyed, once each quarter, over a one-year period. A subsample, approximately 10 percent of the total sample, will be the subject of a more intensive study of intrafamily food distribution. In Rajasthan, a longitudinal survey will be undertaken in which 15 villages will be selected where dairy cooperatives have not been established but where there is an intention to do so about a year after the study has started.

The first stage of this survey will be a complete enumeration of the population, which will include details of land and cattle holdings. From the resulting list, a sample of approximately 700 households will be drawn, which will be interviewed every two months over a three-year period. This survey will, therefore, allow comparisons to be made over time for the same households and will attempt to capture any effects on the acquisition of cattle and land and any social changes that the formation of cooperatives have induced. It will also allow seasonal variations in household income and consumption patterns to be examined. The different nature of the surveys—one cross-sectional, the other longitudinal—will thus provide a basis for measuring project effects in the short and relatively long terms. For both surveys, the analysis will attempt to estimate the contribution of each direct effect of the project to the income, consumption, and nutrition variables. This will include the identification of the principal linkages and the estimation of related key parameters. It is anticipated that, throughout the survey and analysis, the number of parameters on which data are collected will be progressively reduced. Project effects would eventually be measured in terms of a few key relationships that can be evaluated by using more modest surveys and techniques than those proposed in this research. These estimated parameters will then be used to test the usefulness of an ex-ante framework.

The analytical framework consists of three main parts. First, the compiling of comparative data on project benefits. Second, the testing of hypotheses, principally through regression and other statistical procedures. Third, the construction of an econometric model of a farm household that will be used to test and evaluate the effect of changes in the value of parameters caused by the project or other influences. The model will have the following elements:

1. Production functions relating inputs (labor by household members, hired labor, and other agricultural inputs) to output of milk and other agricultural products.

2. Labor demand functions estimated from the production functions.
3. Labor supply functions for individual household members in milk and other production activities.
4. Demand functions for individual household members for home produced and purchased food.
5. Estimated weights for the distribution of commodities within the family.

Responsibility: South Asia Projects Department—Odin K. Knudsen and Roger H. Slade, in collaboration with Per Pinstrup Andersen of the International Food Policy Research Institute. In India, the Institute of Social and Economic Change, Bangalore, and the monitoring and evaluation units of the Rajasthan Cooperative Dairy Federation and the Karnataka Dairy Development Corporation will be the main collaborating institutions. The principal consultant is Pan A. Yotopoulos of Stanford University.

Completion date: October 1984.

Market and Agricultural Policy Determinants of Rural Incomes

Ref. No. 672–39

Most studies of the effects on rural incomes of agricultural growth and technical progress have concentrated on changes in the distribution of incomes among farms of different sizes, resulting from different ways of adopting new farm technology in the adoption cycle and from different modes of access to production credit or irrigation facilities. While these effects are undoubtedly important, the effects of agricultural growth on food prices, wages, and real labor incomes have not been dealt with adequately, although these may be of equal, or greater, significance as determinants of the distribution of income.

A study designed to analyze such issues would have to adopt an approach focusing on price and wage determinants at a more aggregative level rather than being based mainly on sample surveys of farming units. This project aims at constructing aggregative models of the agricultural sector in India and the Philippines that will then be used to analyze the effects of agricultural development policies and projects, trends in population and the labor force, and technical change, on the incomes of major socioeconomic groups. The groups are differentiated by (1) ownership of assets and source of income, (2) supply behavior of factors of production (e.g., labor), (3) expenditure patterns, and (4) location of residence. Although the models are designed to handle a large set of issues related to agriculture, they are intended primarily to examine how the incomes of poor laborers and residents of lagging regions can be improved by rural sector policies and programs. Such programs include rural works, investments in irrigation, agricultural mechanization, input subsidies, agricultural research, and changes in the international trade regime governing agricultural commodities and inputs.

In the models, factor and output prices will be determined endogenously. They are similar in approach to much of the work so far supported by the World Bank on computable general equilibrium models, but differ from it in their emphasis on the econometric estimation of parameters and also by their focus on income distribution and policy issues within a single sector of the economy.

The project complements and draws upon other research at the Bank, including "Evaluation of Food Distribution Schemes" and "India: Impact of Agricultural Development on Employment and Poverty" (Ref. Nos. 671–80 and 671–89, respectively, in this category) and "Wage and Employment Trends and Structures in Developing Countries" (Ref. No. 671–84), now completed.

Responsibility: Development Economics Department—Hans Binswanger, in collaboration with Jaime Quizon and Devendra Gupta of the Institute of Economic Growth, New Delhi (consultants).

Completion date: July 1983.

Canal Command Model for Project Design and System Operation in the Indus Basin

Ref. No. 672-50A

This project is a research application of the project "Programming and Designing Investment: Indus Basin" (Ref. No. 671–45 in this category). Its objectives will be (1) to assist in the design and evaluation of the planned "Command Water Management (CWM)" project and (2) to help develop the analytical capability of the collaborating institution, the Water and Power Development Authority (WAPDA) of Pakistan, for effective system management and planning.

The Command Water Management project is primarily intended to bring about a substantial increase in agricultural production in selected pilot areas through improved water management backed up by the necessary agricultural supporting services and nonwater inputs. The proposed application involves modifying the present Indus Basin modeling system to make it suitable for use in evaluating and planning components of the CWM project. It is intended that these modifications will be made by officers of WAPDA who would thereby acquire experience in using, modifying, and adapting the model system, including its dissemination among other concerned agencies.

Specifically, the research task is to build a canal command model using components of the Indus Basin Model. The model will be used to study losses in flows from the diversion point (barrage) to the fields, additions to and subtractions from the aquifer, and farmer response to additional water and related inputs in terms of increased agricultural production. The data base for the application is unusually good, being the product of an extensive data gathering exercise over the past several years.

The final output of the application will consist of:

1. Inputs into the CWM project, particularly planning the set of components within subprojects, and the evaluation of subprojects.
2. A canal command model that can be used by WAPDA for optimal management of the system and purposes of investment appraisal.
3. An enhanced modeling capability of WAPDA.
4. A slender monograph on the application of modeling techniques to the design and appraisal of irrigation projects at the canal command level. This will be in the nature of a manual addressed to the practitioner.

Responsibility: Development Research Center—John H. Duloy, Gerald T. O'Mara, and Alexander Meeraus, in collaboration with Anthony Brooke (consultant). The major collaborating institution is the Water and Power Development Authority of Pakistan, which will provide two staff members who will be involved in building and applying the canal command model under the supervision of staff of the Development Research Center.

Completion date: June 1982.

4

Industry

Scope for Capital-Labor Substitution in the Mechanical Engineering Industry

Ref. No. 670-23

The Development Research Center has conducted two investigations of planning methodology in the mechanical engineering industries. They have demonstrated the feasibility of implementing numerically solvable process analysis models of mechanical engineering activities (see Ref. No. 670-24 hereunder). The present study extends this methodology to permit the specification of alternative production techniques and the incorporation of product differentiation. It analyzes the scope for capital-labor substitution in mechanical engineering activities and the extent of substitution between locally produced and imported mechanical engineering products.

The first part of this study is concerned with alternative production techniques for given product specifications. The traditional approach of econometric production function analysis is not employed. Instead, to avoid ambiguities that arise through aggregation, process analysis models based on engineering data are constructed for four products: a specific model each of an electric motor, water pump, distribution transformer, and bicycle.

Each product is reduced to its components and subassemblies. The production of each component and each assembly stage is further broken down into a sequence of process stages, i.e., elementary operations performed jointly by labor and a single piece of equipment. Alternative techniques, described by engineers' estimates, are then enumerated at each process stage. For given factor prices, including the cost of capital and wages for different levels of skills, cost minimization determines the optimal technique for each individual process stage at different scales of output. This approach can analyze the sensitivity of optimal production techniques to factor prices, economies of scale, joint production and output mix, the sequential nature of production, and the degree of capacity utilization. Initial results indicate that there is substantial scope for capital-labor substitution in the production of these goods. The optimal choice of technique appears more sensitive to the scale of output than to factor prices, with highly labor-intensive techniques being chosen at low scales and highly mechanized techniques at high scales.

The second part of this study is concerned with substitution between domestically produced and imported textile-weaving machinery in the Republic of Korea. This part of the study is also highly disaggregated in order to isolate the effects of differentials in labor skills, characteristics of individual machines, learning by doing, depreciation and obsolescence, firm organization, and product differentiation. Engineering production functions are estimated econometrically from data at the man-machine level in order to establish relationships between inputs and outputs. (In turn, the structure of prices for differentiated material inputs and outputs is determined using hedonic regression techniques, so that the impact of market structure and certain government incentive policies may be isolated.)

Technique choices are investigated by simulation to obtain the present value of the stream of net revenues associated with particular machines and product mixes. Results (see the fourth report listed below) confirm that substantial scope for capital-labor substitution exists in textile weaving by choosing the degree of automation. For most product mixes, domestically produced machinery is optimal if shadow prices are used and perfect competition is assumed. On the other hand, producers have, in many cases, actually chosen more highly automated imported machinery because of incentives granted by the government, including access to suppliers' credit at lower interest rates, accelerated depreciation, and tariff-exempt imports of machinery. Government incentives in the product markets appear to have altered the mix of products being produced. The hypothesis that producers are profit maximizers is tested and not found to be invalid.

Responsibility: Development Research Center and *Development Economics Department*—Yung W. Rhee, in collaboration with

Larry E. Westphal and with engineers of the Korea Institute of Science and Technology.

Completion date: June 1982.

Reports

Korea Institute of Science and Technology. "Final Report on a Study of the Scope for Capital-Labor Substitution in the Mechanical Engineering Sector." (F6–400–2) February 1973.

Rhee, Yung W., and Westphal, Larry E. "Choice of Technology: Criteria, Search, and Interdependence." In Herbert Giersch (ed.), *International Economic Development and Resource Transfer: Workshop 1978* (Institut für Weltwirtschaft, Kiel). Tübingen: J.C. Mohr (Paul Siebeck), 1979. Also World Bank Reprint Series: Number 103.

———. "Microanalytic Aspects of Complementary Intraindustry Specialization." Paper presented at the seminar on North-South Complementary Intraindustry Trade, Mexico City, August 1980. Summary in *Directors Report*, U.N. 1980, UNCTAD/MD/III, pp. 17–19.

———. "A Micro-Econometric Investigation of Choice of Technology." *Journal of Development Economics* 4 (September 1977):205–237. Also World Bank Reprint Series: Number Fifty.

Westphal, Larry E. "Research on Appropriate Technology." *Industry and Development* 2 (1978):28–46. Also World Bank Reprint Series: Number Eighty-eight.

Programming in the Manufacturing Sector

Ref. No. 670–24

This research project deals with the problem of investment analysis in industries characterized by increasing returns to scale. The study focuses on improved methods for selecting investment projects from among the many alternatives in size, timing, location, technology, and output mix. The research aims at providing operationally useful and practical techniques of analysis that will permit a more systematic treatment of the problem of project selection.

The research effort was begun with three empirical studies, dealing with the Eastern African fertilizer industry, the Korean mechanical engineering industry, and the Mexican heavy electrical equipment industry. In the case of the first two, mixed-integer programming models were formulated in a process-analysis format which made possible an explicit recognition of various forms of interdependence within the sectors. The third study focused exclusively on the methodological problems involved in the modeling of a sector characterized by a large number of products and processes. Aggregation procedures that might be employed in such cases were developed and tested. The Korean study used some of the concepts developed in the Mexican study. The results of this analyis will be published in a monograph, entitled *Industrial Investment Analysis under Increasing Returns*, that will include a detailed and comprehensive statement of the methodology of planning in the presence of increasing returns.

In addition to the monograph, a number of separate volumes addressed to the prospective user of the planning methodology are being published under the series title The Planning of Investment Programs (see under "Reports" below). The series includes volumes on general methodology; investment planning in specific industrial sectors; and detailed guidelines on the use of specifically developed computer software to organize the input data, generate the appropriate planning models, and report on the results. All volumes in the series will be self-contained and will not assume prior familiarity with mathematical modeling, computer languages, or the industrial processes concerned. In addition to a general section, each volume dealing with a specific sector will contain a detailed report on an application of the methodology.

Except for the development of software, the major emphasis of this research program has gradually shifted from research to application and dissemination. Applications are carried out in various contexts. Investment planning studies were completed for the fertilizer sector in the Arab Republic of Egypt, as well as in member countries of the Association of South East Asian Nations (ASEAN) and the Andean Common Market. A detailed case study on India is under way. A planning study is being made of the Mexican steel industry jointly with Mexican counterparts. The World Pulp and Paper Program of the Food and Agriculture Organization (FAO) has used the planning methodology to analyze national and multicountry investment programs in the forest industry sector. Most studies are conducted in collaboration with staff from the World Bank's Industrial Projects Department and relevant regional offices, and usually involve local institutions as well. The Andean Common Market study involved staff and financing from the Junta del Acuerdo de Cartagena and the Inter-American Development Bank.

Responsibility: Development Economics Department and *Development Research Center*—Ardy Stoutjesdijk and Alexander Meeraus, respectively, in collaboration with Yung W. Rhee and Larry E. Westphal, Development Economics Department; Armeane M. Choksi, East Asia and Pacific Regional Office; William F. Sheldrick and Harald Stier, Industrial Projects Department; and Hans Bergendorff, David Kendrick, Peter Glenshaw, Loet Mennes, and Jaime Alatorre (consultants).

Completion date: July 1982.

Reports

Balassa, Bela, and Stoutjesdijk, Ardy. "Economic Integration among Developing Countries." *Journal of Common Market Studies* 186 (September 1974):37–55. Also World Bank Reprint Series: Number Thirty.

Choksi, Armeane; Kendrick, David; Meeraus, Alexander; and Stoutjesdijk, Ardy. *La Programmation des investissements industriels—Méthode et étude de cas.* Paris: Economica, 1981.

Choksi, Armeane, and Meeraus, Alexander. "A Programming Approach to Fertilizer Sector Planning." World Bank Staff Working Paper No. 305. November 1978.

Choksi, Armeane M.; Meeraus, Alexander; and Stoutjesdijk, Ardy. *The Planning of Investment Programs in the Fertilizer Industry.* Volume 2 in the series The Planning of Investment Programs. Baltimore and London: The Johns Hopkins University Press, 1980.

———. "A Planning Study of the Fertilizer Sector in Egypt." World Bank Staff Working Paper No. 269. July 1977.

Kendrick, David, and Stoutjesdijk, Ardy. *The Planning of Industrial Investment Programs, A Methodology.* Volume I in the series The Planning of Investment Programs. Baltimore and London: The Johns Hopkins University Press, 1978.

Stoutjesdijk, Ardy, and Westphal, Larry E. (eds.). *Industrial Investment Analysis under Increasing Returns.* New York: Oxford University Press (forthcoming).

Industrial Policies and Economic Integration in Western Africa

Ref. No. 670-87

Studies on incentives in developing countries have so far concentrated on countries that have already established an industrial base. This research project examines the policies followed by four developing Western African nations that are representative of the region and provide diversity in industrial development, location, and language: Ghana, Ivory Coast, Mali, and Senegal. The purpose of the project is to examine the choice of alternative strategies for economic growth in Western Africa, such as import substitution, export promotion, and the expansion of intraregional trade through economic integration. Attention is given to the choice between the expansion of agriculture or industry in the individual countries. A comparison of the results for the four countries will also shed light on the possibilities for regional integration.

The country studies describe the incentives applied, including tariffs, quantitative restrictions, export taxes and subsidies, tax holidays, credit preferences, and government expenditures. These incentives will be quantified in an effort to gauge their impact on particular industries, or import substitution and exports, as well as on domestic and foreign investment. Information on individual firms and products will also be used to assess the economic cost of the incentive scheme applied, the comparative cost position of various industries, and the benefits of foreign investment.

Indicators of incentives, including the coefficients of effective protection and subsidy, relate the combined effects of measures of protection, and of protective credit, tax and expenditure measures, respectively, to the net gain in foreign exchange in particular activities. These indicators are calculated separately for import substitution and for exports, with further distinction made between preferential and nonpreferential export sales.

Measures of domestic resource costs relate the shadow value of domestic resources used in a particular activity to the net gain in foreign exchange. They are adjusted to take account of the foreign exchange cost of expatriates and of foreign-owned firms, and are also calculated for the case of full capacity utilization and excluding the forgone costs of capital investment.

The final output of the project, which is being carried out by

the Development Research Center in cooperation with the
Western Africa Regional Office, will be a series of country studies and a comparative analysis of the results for the individual
countries. All the country studies have been undertaken with the
support of, and preliminary results have been discussed with, the
governments concerned.

Responsibility: Development Research Center—Bela Balassa.
The individual country studies have been undertaken by the fol-
lowing collaborators: Agricultural sections in all country stud-
ies—J. Dirck Stryker, Tufts University. Industrial sections and
general evaluation: Ghana—Scott R. Pearson and Gerald C.
Nelson, both of the Food Research Institute, Stanford University;
Ivory Coast—Garry Pursell, Industrial Development and Finance
Department, and Terry D. Monson, formerly of the Centre ivoi-
rien de recherche économique et sociale, Abidjan; Mali—
Geoffrey Shepherd, University of Sussex, United Kingdom;
Senegal—Brendan Horton (consultant) and Gary Pursell, Devel-
opment Research Center.

Completion date: June 1982.

Reports

Balassa, Bela. "Avantages comparés et perspectives de l'intégra-
    tion économique en Afrique de l'Ouest." Paper prepared for
    the Colloque sur l'intégration en Afrique de l'Ouest, Dakar,
    Senegal, March–April 1978.
———. "The 'Effects Method' of Project Evaluation." *Oxford
    Bulletin of Economics and Statistics* (November 1976):219–232.
    French translation in *Annales économiques* 11 (1977). Also
    World Bank Reprint Series: Number Fifty-five.
Monson, Terry D., and Pursell, Garry. "An Evaluation of Expa-
    triate Labor Replacement in the Ivory Coast." Discussion
    Paper No. 49. Ann Arbor: University of Michigan, Center for
    Research on Economic Development, April 1976. French
    translation in *L'Actualité économique* (June 1977). Revised ver-
    sion in *Journal of Development Economics* 6 (1979):119–139.
Pursel, Garry. "Cost-Benefit Analysis of Foreign Capital and Ex-
    patriates in the West African Community." Paper presented at
    the International Conference on the Economic Development
    of the Sahelian Countries, Montreal, Canada, October 1977.

A Comparative Study of the Sources of
Industrial Growth and Structural Change

Ref. No. 671-32

Policy appraisal requires an analysis of how policy instruments and autonomous elements interact to determine the allocation of resources. Significant advances have been made over the past decade in understanding the impact of individual government policies operating through price incentives and direct interventions, especially with respect to foreign trade and allocation of investments. But, in the absence of a comprehensive analytical framework for quantitative analysis, few attempts have been made to establish explicit relationships between individual policy instruments, changes in industrial structure, and economic performance. This project will contribute to the development of the analytical framework required to articulate these relationships.

Specifically, the present project is intended to provide the empirical basis, from which quantitative models for policy analysis may be developed in subsequent projects. The relative contributions of growth of domestic demand, export expansion, import substitution, and technological change to industrial growth and structural change, using input-output data, are being determined for Colombia, Israel, Japan, Republic of Korea, Mexico, Norway, Taiwan, Turkey, and Yugoslavia.

In addition to examining changes in the structure of quantities and factor productivities, several studies are investigating changes in the structure of relative prices through deflating the input-output data to the prices of a common base year. Correlations between changes in the structures of quantities and prices will later be used to test various hypotheses concerning the relationship and interaction over time of these variables. The output of this project will include some case studies and a comparative analysis that will appraise the significance of the different industrial incentive policies and development strategies followed.

Parellel to the case studies, a simulation model has been developed to assess the relative importance of universal and economy-specific influences on industrial structure and its evolution. In this model, regression analysis, based on the results of the research project "Patterns of Industrial Development" (Ref. No. 671-05), now completed, is used to provide estimates of the share of the various aggregate demand categories and trade (exports and imports) in gross domestic product (GDP), and of the sectoral disaggregation of each of these as functions of per capita income and size of the area. An input-output matrix, the coefficients of which are obtained from comparative analysis and are dependent upon per capita income, is then used to determine the associated production levels by sector. A simulation for given per capita income, population size, and trade orientation isolates the impact of autonomous factors that are not specific of a given area.

A subsequent project, "The Sources of Growth and Productivity Change: A Comparative Analysis" (Ref. No. 671–79 in this category), involving construction of specific models for several of the areas covered in the first phase, has been initiated to exploit recent advances in the incorporation of policy instruments explicitly within planning models. Each model will be validated by ensuring that it adequately simulates the past history of an area's industrial development. The model will then be used to explore the probable consequences of having followed alternative policies through a series of *ex post* "what if" experiments. Here, as throughout the entire program of research, the emphasis will be on an evaluation of import substitution and export promotion strategies from a long-term, sector-by-sector perspective, stressing questions of sequencing as well as problems of transition to a flexible, viable industrial structure.

Responsibility: Development Economics Department—Sherman Robinson, in collaboration with Hollis B. Chenery and Larry E. Westphal, and with Moises Syrquin of Bar Ilan University (Israel), who are responsible for the overall design of the research and its execution. Tsunehiko Watanabe of the University of Osaka (Japan) also participated in overall supervision until his untimely death in late 1976.

Responsibility for the component parts of the project: Comparative analysis—Hollis B. Chenery and Moises Syrquin; Colombia—Jaime de Melo, Development Economics Department; Israel—Mordechai Fraenkel, Bank of Israel, Jerusalem; Japan—Hollis B. Chenery, Yuji Kubo, and the late Tsunehiko Watanabe; Korea—Kwang Suk Kim, Korea Development Institute, Seoul; Mexico—Moises Syrquin; Norway—Bela Balassa, Development Research Center; Taiwan—Wan-Yong (Shirley) Kuo, National Taiwan University, Taipei; Turkey—Merih Celasun, Middle East Technical University, Ankara.

Completion date: June 1982.

Reports

Balassa, Bela. "Accounting for Economic Growth: The Case of Norway." *Oxford Economic Papers* 3 (November 1979): 415–436. Also World Bank Reprint Series: Number 132.

Chenery, Hollis B. "Transitional Growth and World Industrialization." Paper presented at the Nobel Symposium on the International Allocation of Economic Activity, Stockholm, Sweden, June 1976.

Chenery, Hollis B., and Syrquin, Moises. "A Comparative Analysis of Industrial Growth." Paper presented at the Fifth World Congress of the International Economic Association on Economic Growth and Resources, Tokyo, Japan, August/September 1977.

Kim, Kwang Suk. "Industrialization and Structural Change in Korea." Mimeo. Korea Development Institute, September 1978.

————. "Relative Price Structure and Industrial Growth Patterns in Korea." Mimeo. Korea Development Institute, July 1980.

Kubo, Yuji, and Robinson, Sherman. "Sources of Industrial Growth and Structural Change: A Comparative Analysis of Eight Countries." Paper presented at the Seventh International Conference on Input-Output Techniques, Innsbruck, Austria, April 1979.

Kuo, Shirley W.Y. "Economic Growth and Structural Change in Taiwan." World Bank, August 1979.

Syrquin, Moises. "Sources of Industrial Growth and Change: An Alternative Measure." Paper presented at the European Meeting of the Econometric Society, Helsinki, Finland, August 1976.

Small-Scale Enterprise Development

Ref. No. 671–59

This research project follows on a World Bank Sector Policy Paper, *Employment and Development of Small Enterprises* (February 1978), and a World Bank Issues Paper, *Rural Enterprise and*

Nonfarm Employment (January 1978). The main conclusion of these papers concerned the substantial importance of small-scale enterprises (SSEs), in both urban and rural areas, as sources of employment and earnings opportunities for low-income groups. In developing countries, over three-quarters of the employment outside agriculture is in small enterprises in the industrial, commercial, and service sectors. Yet, it is broadly true that policies concerned with the development of these sectors devote very limited attention and resources toward the development of small-scale enterprises, while little information is available on the nature and functioning of small enterprises and on the constraints and difficulties they face in maintaining or expanding earnings.

The project has two objectives: first, to review the existing information on small enterprises in developing economies and, through trial surveys, to attempt to define ways in which the information base can be improved; and second, to develop a basis, in the course of this work, for assessing the impact on incomes and employment of various policy options.

The research consists of:

- Case studies of patterns of small-scale enterprise development (using existing information) in Colombia, India, Japan, Republic of Korea, Nigeria, the Philippines, and Taiwan.
- A number of surveys of enterprises in manufacturing subsectors in India and Colombia to investigate entrepreneurial history, markets, capital structure, labor use, and other aspects and problems of SSEs.

The case studies also include some analysis and evaluation of policy. The surveys concentrate on about a dozen manufacturing sectors (specified at the five-digit or six-digit level) to gain detailed insights into the workings of the enterprises, their levels of efficiency, and the process of technological transformation and modernization with market development. The surveys are not, however, being restricted solely to small enterprises; interviews with medium and large enterprises are to be undertaken to examine relative efficiency, market competition, and linkages (e.g., through subcontracting).

A further issue that is being examined concerns estimation of the costs and benefits of various policies toward SSEs. It is already apparent that, for example, the implementation of credit and technical assistance programs can be quite costly in relation to the economic benefits generated. Also, a large number of small enterprises exists as an inefficient by-product of policies that depress the demands for labor in agriculture and the 'modern' industrial and commercial sectors. Both these considerations make it important to develop methodology to assess the economic efficiency of policies toward small-scale enterprises.

The major outputs of this research (in addition to a number of individual reports) will be three country monographs—on the Philippines, Colombia, and India—by the principal researchers on the project, which are listed below, and an overall analytic monograph, to be written by Ian Little in collaboration with the other principal researchers.

Responsibility: Development Economics Department—Mark W. Leiserson, Dennis Anderson, Mariluz Cortes, and Dipak Mazumdar, in collaboration with the relevant regional offices in the World Bank, and with José F. Escandon (researcher) from Colombia, Hermina Fajardo (engineer/management consultant) in the Philippines, and R. Albert Berry and John Page (consultants). Ian Little is an adviser to the project.

The following government and research institutions are collaborating in the research: Philippines—Ministry of Industry; India—Sri Ram Center for Industrial Research, New Delhi, and the Giri Institute, Lucknow; Colombia—Corporación Financiera Popular.

Completion date: June 1982.

Reports

Anderson, Dennis. "Small Enterprises and Development Policy in the Philippines: A Case Study." Division Paper No. 66 (Revised June 1981). World Bank: Employment and Rural Development Division, Development Economics Department, June 1981.

Berry, Albert, and Pinell-Siles, Armando. "Small-Scale Enterprises in Colombia: A Case Study." Division Paper No. 56. World Bank: Employment and Rural Development Division, Development Economics Department, July 1979.

Cortes, Mariluz; Ishaq, Ashfaq; and Escandon, José. "Determinants of Economic Performance and Technical Efficiency in Colombian Small and Medium Enterprises." Draft. World Bank: Economics of Industry Division, Development Economics Department, January 1981.

Ho, S.P.S. "Small-Scale Enterprises in Korea and Taiwan."
World Bank Staff Working Paper No. 384. April 1980.

Kaneda, Hiromitsu. "Development of Small and Medium Enterprises and Policy Response in Japan: An Analytical Survey."
Division Paper No. 52. World Bank: Employment and Rural Development Division, Development Economics Department, October 1980.

Mazumdar, Dipak. "A Descriptive Analysis of the Role of Small-Scale Enterprises in the Indian Economy." Draft. World Bank: Employment and Rural Development Division, Development Economics Department, December 1979.

Page, John. "Firm Size, The Choice of Technique and Technical Efficiency: Evidence from India's Soap Manufacturing Industry." Division Paper No. 59. World Bank: Employment and Rural Development Division, Development Economics Department. December 1979.

Managerial Structures and Practices: Public Manufacturing Enterprises

Ref. No. 671-71

Government-owned and government-managed enterprises form a significant and growing segment of the industrial sector in a number of developing countries. This project proposes to examine the degree to which the performance of such enterprises, in relation to their explicit or implicit objectives, depends upon their managerial and organizational structures and the policy environment in which they operate. The broad purpose of this research is to identify the characteristics of the structures and the policy environment that are consistent with the efficiency and growth of such enterprises.

Utilizing the analytical framework of the literature on the economics of industrial organization, and drawing on organization theory and the management sciences, two developing countries—India and Yugoslavia—have been studied. Case studies of three or four public manufacturing enterprises from the same broad subsector in each country formed the core of the research. In addition, a study of the experience of a developed country—Italy—with respect to the management, control, and performance of its public manufacturing enterprises is also a part of the research. Finally, an examination of the evolution of the control environment for public enterprises in India has been undertaken.

The research has made extensive use of interviews and a set of specific hypotheses has been examined, using both quantitative and qualitative evidence. In view of the complexity of the subject matter and the exploratory nature of the proposed effort, the contribution of the study to the operations of the World Bank must be viewed from a long-term perspective. The study is expected, nonetheless, to strengthen the Bank's ability (1) to deal with the issues of management, organization, and policy environment that arise in its lending to industries in the public sector; (2) to address important issues in the public enterprise sector in country economic analysis and sector work; and (3) to respond to technical assistance requests by member governments on various issues of management, organization, and accountability in public sector enterprises. The developing countries participating in this study are expected to benefit not only from a systematic study of their own experiences in the management of public sector industries, but also from the experience of other countries that will be made available to them by the proposed research.

Responsibility: Development Economics Department—Gobind T. Nankani; *Economic Development Institute*—Vinayak V. Bhatt; and *Europe, Middle East, and North Africa Regional Office*—J. Khalilzadeh-Shirazi, with the assistance of Martin Schrenk in the *East Asia and Pacific Regional Office*. Collaborating are P.N. Khandwalla and B.H. Dholakia of the Indian Institute of Management, Ahmedabad, S. Murthy of the Institute of Rural Management, Anand (India), and Romano Prodi of the Center of Economic and Industrial Policy, University of Bologna (Italy) (consultants); and the International Center for Public Enterprises in Developing Countries, Ljubljana (Yugoslavia).

Completion date: All the country studies have been completed in draft form. A final report that will synthesize the three country studies and summarize their findings is expected to be completed by March 1982.

Reports

The following reports are available from the Public Finance Division, Development Economics Department:

Bhatt, V.V. "Decision Making in the Public Sector: A Case Study of Swaraj Tractor." Domestic Finance Studies No. 48. February 1978.

Schrenk, M. "Managerial Structures and Practices in Public Manufacturing Enterprises: A Yugoslav Case Study." World Bank Staff Working Paper No. 455. May 1981.

Appropriate Industrial Technology (Phase II)

Ref. No. 671-77

This project examines the issue of choice of appropriate industrial technology as the problem appears to a lending institution. The study follows Phase I (Ref. No. 671-51), now completed, which quantified the effects of the appropriate choice of technology for employment and national income originating in manufacturing in a typical developing country. For a given level of investment, it was found that these effects are very significant. But the empirical studies upon which these results were based are not sufficiently detailed, particularly with respect to technical engineering issues, to permit their use in project design and evaluation. Moreover, critical issues concerning operating efficiency and industrial organization have typically not been considered. This project attempts to bridge these gaps between the existing state of the art and the needs of project decision makers.

Three related areas are being analyzed:

1. There will be an exhaustive delineation, with the aid of textile engineers, of technical options for the production of blended cotton textiles. Equipment produced in both developed and developing countries will be included in the analysis, and an efficient set of engineering production alternatives defined.

2. The technical production relations determined in part (1) are likely to be altered in actual operation by a number of factors that cause operating efficiencies to differ from those specified by engineering norms. Such inefficiencies may exert different effects on the social profitability of the various technologies and alter the choice of optimum technology. A description and analysis of the nature of operating inefficiencies will be carried out for a number of textile plants in two countries—Kenya and the Philippines—whose economic and physical environments differ.

3. The effects of alternative organizations of production within the sector will be analyzed, particularly as regards the efficiency and feasibility of decentralizing production opera-

tions not subject to economies of scale. The implications of decentralizing production will be considered along with the potential infrastructure and skills required for such dispersal.

The analytical framework to be developed in this project will be suitable for examining technological choices in other industries and in other economic and physical circumstances.

Responsibility: Development Economics Department and *Industrial Projects Department*—Yung W. Rhee and Magdi R. Iskander, respectively, with the collaboration of Howard Pack (consultant).

Completion date: December 1981.

The Sources of Growth and Productivity Change: A Comparative Analysis

Ref. No. 671-79

The objective of this research project is to provide a careful quantitative and comparative analysis of industrialization and growth in selected developing economies. In the first year, analysis will start in the Republic of Korea and Turkey, and a third country may be included after an evaluation of work in the first two. The project is related to an earlier ongoing research project, "A Comparative Study of the Sources of Industrial Growth and Structural Change" (Ref. No. 671-32 in this category).

The earlier project will provide a detailed analysis of the relative importance of domestic demand growth, export expansion, import substitution, and technological change as components of industrial growth in Colombia, Israel, Japan, Republic of Korea, Mexico, Norway, Taiwan, and Turkey. The present project aims at extending and deepening the methodology of comparative analysis by proceeding in two overlapping phases.

In the first phase, a consistent time series of factor inputs and sectoral outputs will be developed, linking the demand-oriented analysis carried out so far to an analysis of the sources of growth from the factor side. In the second phase, a general equilibrium framework of comparative modeling will be used to integrate the analysis of the interactions of sources of growth and policy.

The approach will be explicitly comparative and will emphasize historical trends in terms of different starting points and different policies. The same analysis will be applied, with the linkage between the demand side, the supply side, and the policy-focused analysis being achieved within the framework of a common general equilibrium model. Most comparative studies available have either concentrated on growth accounting from the factor side or on trade and incentive policies. Integrating these two concerns, however, is crucial for a correct evaluation of policy and a comprehensive analysis of the sources of growth.

The same model structure will be applied to all countries, although not only government policies but also the economic behavior simulated may differ by country, reflecting different institutions and socioeconomic settings. The aim is not to build three country models, but to extend the comparative methodology and data base developed in the earlier project on sources of industrial growth to allow for a more formal policy-oriented comparative analysis of industrialization processes. The general equilibrium modeling framework will help to ensure consistency, comparability, and rigor in the analysis.

Responsibility: Development Economics Department—Sherman Robinson and Mieko Nishimizu.

Completion date: June 1982.

Reports

The following papers are available from the Economics of Industry Division, Development Economics Department:

de Melo, Jaime; Kubo, Yuji; Lewis, Jeffrey D.; and Robinson, Sherman. "Multisector Planning Models and Analysis of Alternative Development Strategies." Mimeo. 1980.

de Melo, Jaime, and Robinson, Sherman. "Trade Adjustment Policies and Income Distribution in Three Archetype Developing Economies." World Bank Staff Working Paper No. 442. December 1980.

———. "Trade Policy and Resource Allocation in the Presence of Product Differentiation." March 1980.

Dervis, Kemal; de Melo, Jaime; and Robinson, Sherman. "A General Equilibrium Analysis of Foreign Exchange Shortages in a Developing Economy." World Bank Staff Working Paper No. 443. January 1981.

Dervis, Kemal, and Robinson, Sherman. "A General Equilibrium Analysis of the Causes of a Foreign Exchange Crisis: Turkey, 1973–77." November 1979.

Krueger, Anne O., and Tuncer, Baran. "Estimating Total Factor Productivity Growth in a Developing Country." July 1980.

Nishimizu, Mieko. "On the Methodology and the Importance of the Measurement of Total Factor Productivity Change: The State of the Art." October 1979.

The Industrial Incentive System in Morocco

Ref. No. 671–85

This project represents an application of research methodology that has been successfully tested on several occasions, particularly in the World Bank's study of economic incentive systems in several Western African countries (see "Industrial Policies and Economic Integration in Western Africa," Ref. No. 671–87, in this category). At the same time, the subject matter will be extended to cover the incentive effects of preferences as applied by the European Economic Community (EEC), the intended reform of the incentive system, the economic evaluation of investment projects by government agencies and development banks, and the overall policies toward the public-enterprise sector. Through a collaborative arrangement with, and substantial funding by, the Government of Morocco, the project also aims at promoting institution building. Finally, the project will be oriented to industrial lending by the World Bank to Morocco.

The project has five parts. Part I consists of estimating indicators of incentives, namely, nominal protection, effective protection, and effective subsidy. These indicators will be used to compare the net effect of incentives for import replacement as against exporting, as between industrial subsectors, and as between firms. Part II will estimate indicators of economic costs and benefits in order to give an indication of the relative economic efficiency of the various firms, subsectors, and sectors. For this purpose, it will be necessary to estimate and use shadow prices rather than market prices. In Part III, the results of incentives and the cost-benefit indicators will be analyzed in relation to various measures of factor intensity (including intensity in the use of capital, skilled labor, and unskilled labor), to employment, foreign ownership, export orientation, and location. In Part IV, the results for each sector will be discussed in more detail, paying attention to developments prior to and since 1974. Cost-benefit calculations for selected new projects in each sector will be evaluated in the light of the results by sector and at the firm level, and policy options for each sector will be discussed.

Based on the overall results of the research, Part V will discuss more general policy options, including policies as regards quantitative import restrictions, tariffs, indirect taxes, the Investment Code, preferential credit, export incentives, price controls, wage policies, employment, public ownership, and administrative aspects of the incentive system. Account will be taken of government objectives other than economic efficiency as defined by the cost-benefit indicators, including objectives relating to income distribution, government savings, decentralization of industry, employment, and the use of indigenous labor and capital. Particular attention will be paid to the possibilities for expanding exports to the EEC, on the one hand, and for diversifying export markets, on the other hand.

The findings of the project will be presented in a series of interim working papers to be discussed with a Moroccan interministerial group. These papers will serve, among other things, as a basis for the preparation of Morocco's long-term development plans and the intended reform of the industrial incentive system.

Responsibility: At the World Bank, supervision is assured by an informal steering committee, including Edmond Y. Asfour and George C. Zaidan of the *Europe, Middle East, and North Africa Regional Office* and Bela Balassa of the *Development Research Center.* Most of the research is carried out in Morrocco by a team, including Brendan Horton (a World Bank consultant) and three Moroccan economists. This team is attached to the Ministry of Industry and is responsible to a committee comprising representatives of the Ministries of Finance and Planning, the Central Bank, and the industrial development institutions in Morocco.

Completion date: December 1981.

Industrial Statistics

Ref. No. 671–92

Studies of the international structure of industrial production presently lack reliable and internationally consistent data at the four-digit level of the International Standard Industrial Classification (ISIC). The only standardized industrial statistics presently available are those reported in the *United Nations Yearbook of Industrial Statistics* and the decennial World Census Program. These data are only standardized at the three-digit level of ISIC, and are far from being consistent across countries and/or over time. Available statistics, therefore, have to be cleaned for each sector survey, major industry financing project, and research project, but such cleaning does not lead to international comparability because an overall system is lacking.

This project will lay the groundwork for providing a clean industrial data base that will be updated regularly. In addition to the data, a guide to coverage and quality will be provided. The data will be consistent with other statistical bases, notably those on trade. Industrial statistics will be presented at the three-digit and, wherever possible, four-digit level of ISIC, on gross output, value added, number of employees, and wages and salaries for about 80 countries. The objective is to overcome the difficulties posed by present inconsistencies that include differences in coverage by size of establishment, between survey/sample data and estimates of total manufacturing in census years, and between surveys and national account statistics, as well as missing years and broken time series.

The advantage of a clean industrial data base can be compared to the impetus given to international trade theory with the establishment of the standardized United Nations trade statistics after World War II. These data, standardized for product groups, consistently adjusted to common currency, and so on, enabled researchers to achieve a degree of concreteness and policy relevance that previously had been impossible. Although industry statistics are not in a pre-World War II state, they are definitely in a "buyer beware" state.

As questions of shifts in the industrial product structure, market penetration, and the potential for industrial exports from developing countries become more important economically and politically, margins of error existing in available statistics become increasingly unacceptable. The data base would make it possible to determine shifts in the developing countries' share in global manufacturing over time, in total and by subgroups. This will reveal the penetration of developing countries' exports of manufactures into various markets, as well as the changing ratios of imports and exports to production in developing countries. More ambitiously, the employment, wage, output, and value added data will provide for studies of factor intensity (by various measures), comparative wage costs, and productivity changes. On a broader scale, the development of a consistent data base on industry is expected to provide the basis for a qualitative advance in economic research in industrial development.

The result of the initial work has been presented in two draft papers, entitled "Methodology for the Standardization of Industrial Statistics" and "Standardization of Industrial Statistics for Developing Countries (Progress Report)." The final output, in which the basic material of the draft papers will be incorporated, will consist of (1) a standardized industrial statistics data base and (2) a reference book, entitled *Industrial Data System: User's Guide and Reference Manual.* The project was extended for eight months to increase both country coverage and time series.

Responsibility: Economic Analysis and Projections Department— Sang Eun Lee and Vasilis Panoutsopoulos. The principal researcher is Professor John Weeks (consultant).

Completion date: November 1981.

A Statistical Analysis of the Efficiency of the Indonesian Manufacturing Sector

Ref. No. 672-12

Developing countries often employ a number of policies that restrict trade or interfere with the free functioning of factor markets. As elsewhere in the developing world, one result of the combination of these restrictive policies in Indonesia is a widely varying level of incentives to industrial processes. The purpose of this research project is to conduct a statistical analysis of the efficiency of the Indonesian manufacturing sector.

There are indications that significant intrasectoral variations in capital/labor and skill/labor ratios exist in most of the country's manufacturing activities. This implies that the social efficiency of producing identical units of output may vary across firms. Thus, a major aspect of the analysis will be to investigate the sources of variation in the social cost of production and its components by relating them to firm and, in certain cases, to sector characteristics. These characteristics will include ownership (foreign, private, and government); location, age, and size of the firm; the nature of the special incentives provided; and barriers to competition and restrictions to international trade.

The objective of the research is to calculate the social benefit-cost indicators for individual Indonesian manufacturing firms and analyze the comparative advantage of alternative industrial activities. An appropriate measure for socially evaluating alternative activities is the domestic resource cost (DRC). By making use of a large and unusual set of existing microeconomic data, DRCs will be calculated for a large number of Indonesian industrial enterprises. Based on econometrically estimated frontier production functions, measured DRCs for individual firms will be decomposed into the social costs of technical inefficiency, the social cost of suboptimal factor proportions, and the domestic resource cost of socially inefficient production. These calculations will be used to rank alternative individual activities to investigate the socially optimal choice of technique and to examine the relationship between domestic resource cost, technical inefficiency, and the characteristics of firms and sectors.

It is expected that results from this study will contribute to the Bank's dialogue with the Government of Indonesia and provide direction to its lending program in the industrial sector.

Responsibility: East Asia and Pacific Country Programs Department—Armeane M. Choksi. The principal researcher is Professor Mark Pitt. The Institute of Economic and Social Research, University of Indonesia, and the Central Bureau of Statistics, Indonesia, are collaborating in the research.

Completion date: December 1982.

Programming in the Manufacturing Sector: A GAMS Application

Ref. No. 672–22A

The research project on "Programming in the Manufacturing Sector" (Ref. No. 670–24 in this category) addressed issues related to the analysis of investments in the presence of increasing returns to scale, with special emphasis on process industries such as fertilizers, forest industries, and steel. With the preparation of a series of manuals, currently under way, this project is being completed. However, in order to promote its wider use, it is believed that a series of field applications *cum* training is required to disseminate the planning methodology effectively to prospective users.

The present project will provide the organizational framework for a number of applications, two of which were recently approved by the Research Committee. The first of these concerns is a model of the Indian fertilizer sector. This model is the product of a joint effort by the World Bank's Development Research Center and the Industrial Projects Department. The Government of India intends to use the model to assist in planning the large investments in fertilizer production and distribution. To transfer the model to India, the Bank will train a nucleus of specialists.

The second application is in connection with the proposed Second Mangoro Forestry Project in Madagascar. The Development Economics Department and the Development Research Center are developing a model with which to evaluate alternatives for processing logs, using data to be collected by a consultant firm charged with producing a feasibility study.

Responsibility: Development Economics Department and *Development Research Center*—Ardy Stoutjesdijk and Alexander Meeraus, respectively.

Analysis of Small-Scale Enterprise Lending in Kenya

Ref. No. 672-34

This project builds upon some of the initial results emerging from the World Bank's research project on "Small-Scale Enterprise Development" (Ref. No. 671-59 in this category), in order to develop operationally useful and effective techniques for screening loans to small enterprises.

Problems inherent in lending to small-scale enterprises have been approached mostly from the point of view of the enterprise and research has been based on data collected from them. The investigations have identified a range of constraints upon the borrowers that have prevented most lending programs from being truly effective. Other studies, focusing specifically on the provision of capital and associated technical assistance, have evaluated the policies and performance of individual lending institutions. A third avenue of inquiry—the one to be explored in this project—focuses narrowly on the lending process and the analysis of differential loan performance.

It seeks to provide an answer to a single question: How can an institution lending to small-scale enterprises discriminate among its customers so as to identify those projects and their entrepreneurs that have the highest probability of success?

There are essentially two steps in the analysis. The first is developing a measure of success for each loan based on some combination of loan repayment performance and other evidence of profitable operation. The second step is correlating this observed performance with various explanatory variables—attributes of either the project or the entrepreneur that have been uncovered by the research project referred to above or elsewhere as likely factors. In this context, relevant questions to be asked include:

- whether the project is a new one or an expansion of an old project;
- whether the industrial activity to which it will contribute is a new one or an already established industry;
- whether the loan is intended predominantly for investment in fixed assets or for working capital.

Other potentially significant characteristics to be tested would consist of: the previous and present occupation of the entrepreneur; the proportion of the entrepreneur's time devoted to the enterprise; the entrepreneur's equity as a proportion of total capital invested; the degree of collateral coverage; the time taken by the lending institution to process the loan; the extent of loan repayment follow-up (letters, visits, legal action) by the lending institution.

The project proposed here is an application of this methodology (employing multiple regression analysis) to the loan portfolio of Kenya Industrial Estates, Ltd., the principal development agency for small industry in Kenya.

Responsibility: Development Economics Department—Mark W. Leiserson. The principal researcher is Professor Peter Kilby, Wesleyan University, in collaboration with the Kenya Industrial Estates Ltd., Nairobi, Kenya.

Completion date: December 1981.

The World Aluminum Industry Study

Ref. No. 672-43A

This research project proposes to investigate in depth the long-term future prospects of the world aluminum industry. The study will assess the long-term trends in production costs and prices; the probable structural shifts resulting from the likely changes in the geographical distribution and production costs of electrical energy and bauxite supplies; and the effects of all these on the supply of and demand for aluminum.

The study develops a linear programming model using the General Algebraic Modeling System (GAMS), developed by the Development Research Center (see Ref. No. 671–58 in category 1. Development Policy and Planning) as the model generator. A similar approach was used in a previous research project "Natural Resources and Planning: Issues in Trade and Investment" (Ref. No. 671–09 in category 2. International Finance and Trade). The proposed study incorporates new advances by endogenizing aluminum prices and will take note of potential technological developments in both the production and consumption of aluminum.

The model will be used to simulate sectoral developments under different assumptions concerning the price of inputs, stripping ratios in bauxite mining, levies and tariffs, and transport costs. Although this approach does not incorporate directly nonquantifiable aspects, such as potential investors' assessment of risks that may occur within a country or market diversification, an attempt will be made to include some of these factors by introducing constraints in some versions of the model.

This research will enhance the Bank's understanding of the economics of the world aluminum industry and provide a framework for analyzing various specific aspects of the industry. Specifically, it will be of fundamental importance to the operational departments of the Bank in their work in evaluating large aluminum plants and power projects related to aluminum production. Finally, for the Development Economics Department, the project represents the first phase in its research on the appraisal methodology for very large projects.

Responsibility: Economic Analysis and Projections Department and *Development Economics Department*—Ardy Stoutjesdijk and Kenji Takeuchi, respectively. The principal researchers are Alfredo Dammert, Economic Analysis and Projections Department, and Alexander Meeraus, Development Research Center, in collaboration with the Industrial Projects Department and the Energy Department, and Martin Brown, Development Center of the Organisation for Economic Co-operation and Development (OECD).

Completion date: October 1981.

Experimental Support Unit for Work on Industrial Incentives and Comparative Advantage (the INCA Unit)

Ref. No. 672–44A

Over the years, a major portion of research on industry in developing countries, supported by the World Bank, has been devoted to the quantitative analysis of incentive systems and comparative advantage (INCA analysis). In the course of this research, a considerable body of knowledge has been built up on all aspects of this kind of analysis. At the same time, there has been a steady increase in the demand for such studies from governments of member countries and operating departments of the Bank, which have increasingly come to perceive these studies to be directly relevant for incentive policy reforms and for increasing the economic efficiency of new investment.

For a considerable time, staff members involved in INCA research have been giving advice and assistance to operational staff responsible for applied INCA studies on an *ad hoc* basis. It has now become apparent that this assistance could be more cost-effective, if it were to some degree formalized by the establishment of a unit that would centralize the needed specialized skills. Accordingly, under this project an Industrial Incentives and Comparative Advantage (INCA) unit has been established on an experimental basis for a two-year period. The unit will work on methodologies and techniques (including computer programs and software), developed in the course of past research in this field, to make them more useful for operational work. It will provide support to operating departments of the Bank and to the International Finance Corporation (IFC).

A major objective of the unit, which is part of the Industrial Development and Finance Department of the Central Projects Staff, would be to assist the regional operating departments in building up the capability of national institutions to undertake INCA analysis.

Apart from support for longer-term studies and the development of more operational techniques, the unit will support INCA-related work at the Bank and IFC by providing methodologies, software and computer programs, information on consultants, and relevant data, including those on international prices. It will also assist industry sector missions (including IFC missions) in analyzing industrial incentives, and will have a role in coordinating the use of shadow prices in sector and project work.

If the experiment is successful, it is envisaged that the work of the unit will be absorbed into and become a permanent part of the activities of the Industrial Development and Finance Department.

Responsibility: Industrial Development and Finance Department—Garry Pursell, in collaboration with the Economics of Industry Division of the *Development Economics Department*, a Bank staff member still to be determined, and Yoon Joo Lee (researcher). The unit will work with a number of consultants and expects to become directly involved in INCA work undertaken by government agencies and research organizations in a number of member countries.

Completion date: August 1983.

The Acquisition of Technological Capability

Ref. No. 672–48

Technological change is now generally recognized as essential to industrial development. In the research community considerable effort has been addressed to issues of choice of technique, appropriate technology, technology transfer, and more recently to technological change at the individual firm level. Nevertheless, there is little understanding of what technological change in developing countries means.

Despite the lack of research that might guide policy, governments in many developing countries have attempted to create local technological capability by intervening directly and indirectly. Partly as a result of these interventions, different developing countries have achieved different levels of technological capability. However, there is no systematic evidence for appraising the success or the benefits of promoting such capability. The sequence of activities a developing country should undertake at different points in its industrial development to build up its technological capability is unclear.

This research project is intended to yield an overview of technological capability in industry to develop an understanding of what technological capability consists of and how it is acquired. It will seek cross-country comparative information, in order to get a broad appreciation of different country experiences and of different relations between local technological capability, industrial development, and government policies. The project has links with other current research at the World Bank on trade and industry. However, it focuses explicitly on technological change and, thus, represents an evolution from past Bank research on technology, which concentrated mostly on choice of techniques.

The initial focus chosen for the cross-country comparative study is exports of technology from developing countries. Technology exports are presumptive evidence of underlying technological capability, while the fact that know-how is being exported gives a *prima facie* indication of world standards of competence. Two pilot studies, already completed, confirm that focusing on technology exports is a useful way of identifying areas where local technological capability has been developed. Technology exports tend to reveal differences between countries in the areas of expertise and in the ways that technological capability has been established.

The study will seek information at two levels. Phase I will map out the extent and nature of technology exports from a selected group of developing countries. Its objectives are to learn what these technology exports indicate about the development of technological capabilities in different countries and its relationship to government policies, and to identify interesting cases or sectors for further study. As tentatively planned, Phase II will study the acquisition of technological capability in some of the sectors identified in Phase I.

The project will cover three countries—India, the Republic of Korea, and Mexico. The Inter-American Development Bank participated in the initial design of this project, and is planning to undertake a similar study in Brazil and perhaps some other Latin American countries.

The project will produce a summary monograph as well as individual country reports. There will also be interim country reports summarizing the results of Phase I and outlining the methodology and strategy for Phase II.

Responsibility: Development Economics Department—Larry E. Westphal and Carl J. Dahlman. Responsibility for the individual country studies is as follows: India—Sanjaya Lal, Oxford Institute of Economics and Statistics; Korea—Alice Amsden, Barnard Col-

lege, and a Korean consultant still to be determined; Mexico—
Carl Dahlman and Mariluz Cortes of the World Bank.

Completion date: Phase I—September 1982; Phase II—January
1984.

Reports

Dahlman, Carl J. "Technology Exports as a Starting Point in the
Study of Technological Capability: The Findings of a Pilot
Study in Brazil and Mexico." Mimeo. April 1981.

Dahlman, Carl J., and Westphal, Larry E. "Technological Effort
in Industrial Development—An Interpretative Survey of Past
Research." July 1981.

Westphal, Larry E.; Rhee, Yung W.; and Pursell, Garry. "Korean
Industrial Competence: Where It Came From." World Bank
Staff Working Paper No. 469. July 1981.

5

Transportation, Water, and Telecommunications

Substitution of Labor and Equipment in Civil Construction

Ref. No. 670–26

Civil works are important for developing countries, but they are often built with equipment-intensive methods, even though there may be an abundant supply of unemployed labor. In 1971, the World Bank launched "The Study of Labor and Capital Substitution in Civil Construction" as a framework for research and implementation related to construction methods that are more appropriate for the socioeconomic environment of labor-abundant and capital-scarce countries.

Phase I of the study (February–October 1971) reviewed the available literature. It established the technical feasibility of factor substitution for a wide range of construction activities. However, a number of variations were noted in productivity rates reported in the literature with respect to both labor and equipment. Hence, Phase I indicated the need for an extensive collection of field data.

Phase II (November 1971–October 1973) collected field data at 30 road, dam, and irrigation sites in India and Indonesia where labor-based construction methods have been used for centuries. Data collection focused on the social, physical, and managerial parameters that might explain variations in labor-equipment productivity. Two major conclusions emerged: (1) as practiced in 1972 in India and Indonesia, traditional labor-based methods were not competitive with modern equipment-based methods; (2) labor productivity (and, hence, improved efficiency and competitiveness) could be markedly improved through better organization and management, through better tools and light equipment, and through the upgrading of the health and nutritional status of the workers.

Phase III (September 1973–August 1976) focused on experimental work in India on both road and irrigation projects and demonstrated the possibility of significant productivity increases through the introduction of improved procedures at the site level. At that point, the importance of the distinction between site and program became evident. A site is one of (possibly) many geographically dispersed points where construction takes place. A program is the aggregation of a number of sites into a plan of action for the improvement of technically similar infrastructure facilities. Programs are conceived and implemented by a central agency that plans, finances, and supervises the work carried out at the individual sites.

Phase III showed that improvements in management, tools, and the health/nutritional status of the labor force could significantly increase productivity at the site level. But it also suggested that improved procedures for planning, financing, staff training, and monitoring of progress should be implemented at the program level, if labor-based methods are to be competitive with equipment at a large scale of operations.

Findings of Phases I and II were summarized in two reports; findings and conclusions from specific aspects of the work of Phase III were summarized in three papers whose appearance marked the beginning of a wider dissemination of study-related material (see under "Reports").

In 1975, the study team initiated a series of Technical Memoranda to report on important or novel aspects of labor-based construction operations. A total of 28 titles has appeared and copies have been distributed through a mailing list numbering over 300 persons (planners, engineers, civil servants, economists, and academics) all over the world.

Starting in 1976, the study team became increasingly more involved in the planning and implementation of labor-based demonstration projects in Benin, Dominican Republic, Honduras, Lesotho, and the Philippines. Dissemination within the Bank of the findings of the study included a three-day seminar in 1977. Dissemination of findings of the study outside the Bank included a series of two-day seminars organized by the study team in Washington, Cologne, Copenhagen, London, and Tokyo, in

May–June 1978. A review of the study appeared in *World Bank Research News* of May 1980, which contains a discussion of the study phases and of the conclusions that emerged from each.

Independently of the study, a report has been prepared with the collaboration of members of the study team on competitive bidding on construction projects in labor-abundant economies. Many governments have embarked on programs of labor-based public works construction out of political and social necessity, ususally without full consideration of the economic factors involved. Because force account operations are readily adaptable to any desired mix of labor and equipment, they have tended to monopolize public works construction in many countries. To improve cost effectiveness and efficiency, a shift in policy by governments toward executing more construction projects by competitive bidding among contractors is desirable, while at the same time retaining and encouraging the opportunities for labor-based operations. This report (listed below) discusses the general requirements of any modified procedure for bid evaluation on construction projects in labor-surplus economies, describes possible alternative procedures for shadow pricing of inputs, and recommends a system using discounted wage rates in bid evaluation as being the most practicable.

Lessons from the research and field work carried out within the context of the study have been summarized in a handbook currently being published. The handbook contains pragmatic guidelines for the planning, execution, and monitoring of labor-based civil construction programs in capital-scarce and labor-abundant developing countries.

Apart from the resources allocated to it by the World Bank, the study has been financially supported by the governments of Denmark, Finland, the Federal Republic of Germany, Japan, Norway, Sweden, the United Kingdom, and the United States.

Responsibility: Transportation, Water, and Telecommunications Department—Helmut S. Kaden. The British consulting firm of Scott, Wilson, Kirkpatrick and Partners and the consulting firm of GITEC in the Federal Repubic of Germany have extensively participated in the study. The Overseas Development Ministry of the United Kingdom has provided a number of specialists who assisted at different stages of the study. Extensive field support has been provided by the governments of Honduras, India, and Kenya.

Completion date: All research and field work has been completed. The handbook will be published shortly.

Reports

Bose, Swadesh R. "Some Aspects of Unskilled Labor Markets for Civil Construction in India: Observations Based on Field Investigation" (Phase III). World Bank Staff Working Paper No. 223. November 1975.

Coukis, Basil P., and others. *Labor-Based Construction Programs: A Planning and Management Handbook.* New Delhi: Oxford University Press, 1981 (forthcoming).

Coukis, Basil P., and Grimes, Orville F., Jr. "Labor-based Civil Construction." *Finance and Development* 17 (March 1980): 32–35.

Harral, Clell G. "Transport Research in the World Bank." *World Bank Research News* 2 (May 1980):1–5.

"A Guide to Competitive Bidding on Construction Projects in Labor-Abundant Economies." Washington and London: World Bank and Scott, Wilson, Kirkpatrick and Partners, 1978.

"Labor-Intensive Construction Techniques: Report of a World Bank Seminar." World Bank: Transportation, Water, and Telecommunications Department, 1977.

"Scope for the Substitution of Labor and Equipment in Civil Construction—A Progress Report" (Phase III). New Delhi: Indian Roads Congress, December 1979.

"Some Aspects of the Use of Labor-Intensive Methods for Road Construction" (Phase III). New Delhi: Indian Roads Congress, December 1976.

"The Study of Labor and Capital Substitution in Civil Engineering Construction: Report on the World Bank-sponsored Seminars in Washington, Cologne, Copenhagen, London, and Tokyo." World Bank: Transportation, Water, and Telecommunications Department, September 1978.

The following papers are out of print but may be consulted in the files of the Transportation, Water, and Telecommunications Department:

Harral, Clell G., et al. "Study of the Substitution of Labor and Equipment in Civil Construction: Phase II Final Report." January 1974.

"Study of the Substitution of Labor and Equipment in Civil
    Construction: Organization and Management Study (Phase
    III)." Chester: CODECON, 1975.
"Study of the Substitution of Labor and Equipment in Road
    Construction: Phase I Final Report." October 1971.
"Study of the Substitution of Labor and Equipment in Civil
    Construction: Phase III Technical Report." Washington and
    London: World Bank and Scott, Wilson, Kirkpatrick and Part-
    ners, 1975.

Highway Design Maintenance Standards Study

Ref. No. 670–27

Assistance by the World Bank for highway development is focused on lower-income, capital-scarce countries with widely varying climates. In these countries, the trade-offs between initial
construction cost and future maintenance and road-user costs
may well dictate highway design and maintenance strategies that
are different from those prevailing in North America and Europe.
Developing countries spend more than $10 billion annually on
their highway systems and much larger amounts for the operation of the vehicles using these highways. Thus, there is a clear
need for research to support an analysis of trade-offs among
major cost components in evaluating alternative highway design
and maintenance standards.

Phase I of the Highway Design Study, completed in 1971,
developed a conceptual framework for analyzing relationships
between design standards, maintenance standards, and vehicle
operating costs. But it concluded that empirical data to estimate
many of the cost relationships necessary to determine optimum
strategies were lacking.

Phase II of the research has, therefore, focused on the collection and analysis of primary data on the underlying physical and
economic relationships necessary to calculate cost trade-offs
under various conditions. A major field study was undertaken in
Kenya from 1971 to 1974 to cover road, traffic, and environmental conditions typical of Eastern Africa. A parallel study in Brazil,
now in its final stages, will extend the data base with respect to
vehicle operating costs and road deterioration (including alternative maintenance policies) for conditions typical of much of Latin
America. Finally, a study of vehicle operating costs in India that

is addressing the special construction methods and traffic patterns encountered there is expected to be completed in 1982.

A significant feature of these field studies is the combination of a road-user survey (which collects comprehensive cost data on vehicle operation, fuel and oil consumption, tire wear, crew costs, and vehicle maintenance, utilization, and depreciation) with experimental work on speed and fuel consumption. The Kenya and Brazil studies have quantified, for the first time, the effects of various road surface conditions on vehicle speeds and operating costs. Relationships have been established between major decision variables (vertical and horizontal alignment, type of road curve, and condition of the road), and vehicle speed, fuel consumption, and certain other components of vehicle operation costs. Also, an improved information base on the deterioration and maintenance of gravel roads and roads with a cement-modified base and double bituminous surface treatment has been developed. Continuing long-term follow-up studies in Kenya and Brazil will yield more complete information on the deterioration of asphalt concrete pavements and alternative overlay designs.

The development of management decision models has paralleled the field research. Most features of two earlier models, developed initially at the Massachusetts Institute of Technology (MIT) and subsequently at the Transport and Road Research Laboratory (TRRL) in the United Kingdom, have now been incorporated in a new model—HDM (Highway Design Maintenance). Costs are obtained by first estimating physical quantities and then applying prices or unit costs; either economic or financial prices may be used. The models are able to determine the total life-cycle transportation costs, provide economic comparisons for large numbers of alternative designs and maintenance policies, and can, thus, be used to search for the lowest total cost alternative.

Designed as a project planning tool, the HDM model is already used at the prefeasibility and feasibility stages of planning in many countries by government agencies and consultants as well as by the World Bank, particularly in the planning of highway maintenance programs. Its use is now being extended to highway sector planning under budget constraints.

Phase III of the study (1980–82) is concentrating on a systematic and comprehensive analysis of the entire new data set. Several publications are planned, including a revised edition of Jan de Weille's *Quantification of Road User Savings* (Baltimore and London: The Johns Hopkins University Press, 1966, 3rd printing 1970, out of print) and a book evaluating the major options in road design and maintenance strategies.

Responsiblity: Transportation, Water, and Telecommunications Department—Clell G. Harral and Thawat Watanatada. The work in Kenya was done by the Transport and Road Research Laboratory of the United Kingdom, in collaboration with the Ministry of Works. The study in Brazil is being undertaken by the Brazilian Transport Planning Agency (GEIPOT), with technical assistance from the University of Texas, Austin, and financial support from the United Nations Development Programme (UNDP). The study in India is being conducted by the Central Road Research Institute, New Delhi, in collaboration with the Indian Institute of Technology, Kanpur, and the Indian Institute of Statistics. The Swedish National Traffic and Road Research Institute (VTI) and the Australian Road Research Board are also providing technical assistance on research of traffic flows.

Completion date: The basic work in Kenya is completed. The HDM computer model, merging most features of the TRRL and MIT models, except the construction cost submodel, is now available. The model is revised and extended as results from ongoing research become available. The study in Brazil, except for long-term monitoring of paved road experiments, will be completed in early 1982 and that in India in late 1982.

Reports

Harral, Clell G., and Agarwal, Surendra. "Highway Design Standards Study." Paper presented at the (First) International Conference on Low Volume Roads. Special Report 160. U.S. Transportation Research Board, 1975.

Harral, Clell G.; Fossberg, Per E.; and Watanatada, Thawat. "Evaluating the Economic Priority of Highway Maintenance." Paper presented at the Pan-African Conference on Highway Maintenance, Accra, Ghana, November 1977.

————. "The Highway Design and Maintenance Standards Model." Paper presented at the Second International Conference on Low Volume Roads, Ames, Iowa, August 1979.

Hide, H., et al. *The Kenya Road Transport Cost Study: Research on Vehicle Operating Costs.* TRRL Laboratory Report 672.

Crowthorne, United Kingdom: Transport and Road Research Laboratory, 1975.

Hodges, J. W., et al. *The Kenya Road Transport Cost Study: Research on Road Deterioration.* TRRL Laboratory Report 673. Crowthorne, United Kingdom: Transport and Road Research Laboratory, 1975.

Moavenzadeh, Fred, et al. "Highway Design Study, Phase I: The Model." World Bank Staff Working Paper No. 96. January 1971 (out of print).

Watanatada, Thawat. "The Highway Design and Maintenance Standards Model: Model Description and User's Manual (Release II)." World Bank: Transportation, Water, and Telecommunications Department, June 1981.

Watanatada, Thawat, and Harral, Clell G. "Determination of Economically Balanced Highway Expenditure Programs under Budget Constraints: A Practical Approach." Paper presented at the World Conference on Transport Research, London, April 1980.

Pricing and Financing of Urban Public Services: Water Supply and Sewage Disposal

Ref. No. 671-18

One of the most important questions of public policy in developing countries is how to finance the provision of public services in rapidly growing urban areas. This research project considers this question for the case of water supply and sewage disposal in two cities—Cali (Colombia) and Nairobi (Kenya). The project is an outgrowth of the World Bank's research on "Urban Public Finance and Administration" (Ref. No. 670-70 in category 7. Urbanization and Regional Development) in which self-financing used was identified as one of the major (and fastest growing) ways of extending urban public services.

In this study, methods are developed for evaluating the trade-offs among the four major policy objectives of pricing of public services: efficiency, equity, fiscal viability, and administrative feasibility. Existing and potential pricing practices are analyzed with respect to their allocative, distributive, and fiscal effects, and their administrative implications. The analysis will be based on investigations of (1) demand and cost conditions for the services considered, at the household and/or neighborhood level;

(2) other major financing techniques, such as general taxation; and (3) administrative arrangements and intergovernmental relations involved in providing the services.

The data on consumption, service charges, tax payments, and cost of service delivery were collected from the local public agencies that provide the services and collect the taxes. Income and other socioeconomic data at the household and neighborhood levels were obtained from existing surveys and from census information.

To date, the research output consists of two background papers—the first on intergovernmental fiscal relations and the second on equity and efficiency in the theory of public utility pricing—and of a number of technical papers reporting on selected research conclusions for Cali and Nairobi. Included are such areas as the determinants of water demand, the costs of water and sewerage systems, and the financial and fiscal structure of urban government. The papers will be reviewed in the final report, which will discuss the implications of alternative pricing strategies in terms of efficiency, equity, and fiscal impact.

Responsibility: Development Economics Department—Johannes F. Linn, in collaboration with Richard M. Bird, L. Kenneth Hubbell, and Charles E. McLure, Jr. (consultant).

Completion date : December 1981.

Reports

Bird, Richard. *Central-Local Fiscal Relations and the Provision of Urban Public Services.* Research Monograph No. 30. Centre for Federal Financial Relations. Canberra: The Australian National University, 1980.

————. "Intergovernmental Fiscal Relations in Developing Countries."World Bank Staff Working Paper No. 304. October 1978.

Hubbell, L. Kenneth. "The Residential Demand for Water and Sewerage Services in Developing Countries: A Case Study of Nairobi." Urban and Regional Report No. 77–14. April 1977.

Linn, Johannes F. "The Distributive Effects of Local Government Finances in Colombia: A Review of the Evidence." In R. Albert Berry and Ronald Soligo (eds.), *Economic Policy and Income Distribution in Colombia.* Boulder, Colorado: Westview Press, 1980. Also World Bank Staff Working Paper No. 235. March 1976.

_____. "Estimation of Water Supply Costs in Cali, Colombia." Urban and Regional Report No. 76-14. September 1976.

_____. "The Incidence of Urban Property Taxation in Colombia." In Roy W. Bahl (ed.), *The Taxation of Urban Property in Less Developed Countries*. Madison: The University of Wisconsin Press, 1979.

_____. "The Incidence of Urban Property Taxation in Developing Countries: A Theoretical and Empirical Analysis Applied to Colombia." World Bank Staff Working Paper No. 264. August 1977.

McLure, Charles E., Jr. "Average Incremental Costs of Water Supply and Sewerage Services: Nairobi, Kenya." Urban and Regional Report No. 77-13. April 1977.

_____. "Public Utility Pricing: Issues in Efficiency and Equity." Urban and Regional Report No. 77-15. May 1977.

The Urban and Regional Reports are available from the Urban and Regional Economics Division, Development Economics Department.

Design and Monitoring Tools for Water Supply and Sanitation

Ref. No. 672-06

This project is conducting exploratory research into the demand for water supply and sanitation. Forecasts of demand are needed to determine the optimal sizing of investments, to construct financial projections, to determine the impact of investments and tariff policies on various income groups, and to assess the magnitude of project benefits.

The project has focused on four topics. The first subproject has examined the theoretical problems in using hedonic price analysis to determine the value of water supply and sanitation services not captured by tariff charges. The approach seeks to infer the value of amenities from the rents for or sales prices of residential properties.

The second subproject has explored econometric problems in estimating the demand for water from cross-sectional data. The analysis has distinguished between the decision to connect to a public water supply and the choice of how much water to consume after having purchased a connection. This subproject has also investigated methods of estimating the demand curve for water from data on a progressive tariff in which rates vary with the quantity being consumed.

The third subproject has examined the empirical relationship between prices and quantities for a number of cities in developing countries. This study has sought to identify empirical regularities rather than to estimate a demand function.

The final subproject has examined the consequences of errors in demand forecasts for the cost of providing water supplies. Both numerical and analytical models have been prepared. These models reveal that because of economies of scale to plant, the costs of excess capacity are modest, while the costs of underinvestment (e.g., planning for too little demand) are substantial.

Responsibility: Transportation, Water, and Telecommunications Department—John M. Kalbermatten and Fredrick L. Golladay, in collaboration with Professors W.M. Gorman, Donald T. Lauria, and Vincent Paqueo (consultants).

Completion date: October 1981.

The Determinants of Railway Traffic, Freight Transport, and the Choice of Transport Modes

Ref. No. 672-07

An in-house review of railways supported by the World Bank revealed some causes of concern in three broad areas: volumes and types of traffic, operating efficiency, and finances. The last two raise institutional questions that are being investigated in the course of the Bank's operational work.

In planning railway investments in developing countries, demand for railway traffic has often been extremely difficult to forecast. Future freight traffic has often been overestimated and passenger traffic has been underestimated, sometimes with unfortunate consequences. The research project on the "Economic Role of Railways" (Ref. No. 671–50), now completed, has investigated determinants of the pace and pattern of shifts between different modes of transportation. Its findings suggest that the share of railways in total freight transport has been declining (despite some increases in absolute volumes); that railways are increasingly becoming specialized carriers used for relatively large shipments over long distances; and that the share of railways has been declining irrespective of the relative prices of different transport modes. But though this research is yielding hypotheses about shippers' choice of modes and the factors governing this choice, the data available do not permit these to be rigorously formulated and tested.

A further phase of research, approved in October 1979, will use information collected by the Netherlands Institute of Transport for a study of freight traffic in the European Economic Communities and Spain, since data are not available in sufficient detail for developing countries. A detailed analysis of this data base should sharpen understanding of the comparative advantage of railways as against other modes of transport in different circumstances and of the factors governing shippers' choice of transport modes, for specified groups of commodities. It is expected to yield rigorously formulated hypotheses that can be tested in studies of individual developing countries.

Responsibility: Transportation, Water, and Telecommunications Department—Pedro N. Taborga and M.S. Nanjundiah. Most of the work will be undertaken by the Netherlands Institute of Transport.

Completion date: Since the major part of the funding for this project has not yet been made available by the Netherlands Government, work on the project has not begun and no completion date has been set.

6
Energy

Standards of Rural Electrification

Ref. No. 671–86

Rural electrification schemes in developing countries are estimated to absorb about $50 billion during the next decade, while
lending by the World Bank in this area will average about $300
million a year over the next few years. Many of the Bank's borrowers, particularly those that are in the early stages of rural
electrification, are looking to the Bank for guidance in this
crucial and capital-intensive area of rural infrastructure. This
research project will help develop a methodology for improving
the efficiency of investments in rural electrification and establish
guidelines that should aid in formulating and appraising projects
in this subsector.

Phase I of the study has been completed and consists of a critical evaluation of design criteria and standards of rural electrification in 12 developing countries. It includes a review of previous
studies and relevant practices in the developed countries and
the results of field trips. Concurrently, a combined economic-
engineering methodology was developed to optimize the design
of a rural electrification network, based on variations in the quality of supply. The approach used in this study considered system
costs as well as costs incurred by consumers due to poor quality
of supply and, therefore, subsumed the conventional criterion in
power system planning of minimizing only the supply costs. All
the usual economic techniques applicable to developing countries—in particular, shadow pricing—were used. Theoretical
models of the activities of various types of electricity users were
also developed.

Phase II of the study is now under way. Following the methodology developed in the first stage, the net economic benefits will be maximized for two rural electrification networks (in India and Costa Rica). Particular attention is being paid to alternative qualities of supply and their impact on the type of usage and on the growth of load. Surveys have been made to verify the accuracy of the theoretical framework of user activity, the value users place on electricity, and the willingness to pay for electricity supply of various qualities.

Responsibility: Energy Department—Mohan Munasinghe, in collaboration with Walter G. Scott (consultant) to assist with the engineering aspects of the study.

Completion date: November 1981.

Reports

Munasinghe, Mohan. "The Optimal Planning of Rural Electric Systems and the Quality of Supply." Paper presented at a Development Policy Staff Microeconomics Seminar. World Bank: Energy Department, May 6, 1980.

Pricing of Indigenous Energy Resources

Ref. No. 672-15

The cost of energy emerged as a major development constraint in the 1970s. The decade ended with the international price of crude oil doubling in a single year to almost $30 per barrel, presaging continued stress during the 1980s. The impact of these increases on the oil-importing developing countries has been well documented, as have their efforts to expand the production of indigenous energy resources. At the same time, there is a growing recognition that demand management policies encouraging conservation and a more efficient use of energy can play an important role in easing energy constraints.

The pricing of energy products, both for project appraisal and for the market place, is a central tool of energy demand management. The optimal choice of project design and development strategy hinges upon the appropriate price of energy inputs in the economy. Thus, in order to promote efficient energy use, decision makers at all levels should be able to identify the energy prices that reflect real present and expected future scarcities.

The first goal of this project is to develop and test a widely applicable methodology for producing such "economic" prices.

The other side of demand management concerns the marginal choices made daily by energy consumers, which involve the market prices of energy products. Such prices have social, financial, and even strategic implications for governments, and often differ from the economic prices that would be appropriate for project decision making. It is important to explore the role that energy pricing policies can have in achieving fiscal, social, and other noneconomic objectives and to assess the costs involved in diverging from strictly "economic" prices. The overall operational purpose of the research is to enable the Bank better to advise and support borrowing countries' strategies for energy demand management.

The research design is essentially one of filling gaps that presently exist between the economic literature on depletable resources and the existing pricing policies, energy technologies, consumption patterns, and data available in developing countries. Thus the project began with a review of the literature that highlighted both areas of substantial agreement and those requiring further definition and empirical study. Since pricing issues cut across both demand and supply questions, the pricing review is also a useful guide to the broader energy literature on developing countries; it contains a bibliography of nearly a thousand references. The second stage of the research involves an empirical analysis of domestic petroleum product prices in some 50 countries over the period 1970–80 and selected case studies to explore the links between opportunity cost pricing, conservation policies, and the use of the energy sector to generate fiscal resources.

Responsibility: Energy Department—DeAnne S. Julius, in collaboration with Meta Systems (consultants).

Completion date: September 1982.

Reports

Julius, DeAnne, and Meta Systems. "Energy Pricing in Developing Countries: A Literature Review." Energy Department Paper. September 1981.

7
Urbanization and Regional Development

Urban Public Finance and Administration

Ref. No. 670-70

Little research has been done on municipal finance and tax systems in developing countries. Nonetheless, this area is of great importance to national and local governments in these countries, as well as to the World Bank, in dealing with the problems of large and rapidly growing cities.

This research project consists of a comparative analysis of selected features of local fiscal systems in nine cities: Ahmedabad and Bombay (India), Bogota and Cartagena (Colombia), Jakarta (Indonesia), Kingston (Jamaica), Manila (Philippines), Seoul (Republic of Korea), and Tunis (Tunisia). Through detailed case studies and a comparative evaluation of these cities, the study attempts to ascertain and analyze the pattern of expenditures and revenues, the adequacy of the overall structure of municipal revenues, and the trade-offs between tax adequacy and tax equity.

The data collected allow the assessment of alternative strategies for financing municipal development. Emphasis is placed on the sharing of authority to collect revenues and responsibility for expenditures between the various levels of government, on the growth potential of alternative sources of revenues, and on the effects on income distribution of differential revenue structures. Attention is also focused on the administrative aspects of budgeting and fiscal planning, taxation and service delivery, and intergovernmental fiscal relations.

The output of the research comprises nine monographs, containing the city case studies, and a comparative report, dealing with urban expenditures and financing needs, property taxation, financing and pricing criteria for self-financed services, and intergovernmental relations. In addition, a number of publications, among them a statement on the role of urban public finance in project preparation, have reported on the results and implications of this research.

Responsibility: Development Economics Department—Johannes F. Linn, in collaboration with Roy W. Bahl (consultant) and assisted by Francine Bougeon-Maassen, Rémy Prud'homme, Roger S. Smith, and Hartojo Wignjowijoto (consultants).

Completion date: December 1981.

Reports

Bahl, Roy W. "The Practice of Urban Property Taxation in Less Developed Countries." In Roy W. Bahl (ed.), *The Taxation of Urban Property in Less Developed Countries.* Madison: The University of Wisconsin Press, 1979.

————. *Urban Property Taxation in Developing Countries.* Occasional Paper No. 32. Metropolitan Studies Program. Syracuse, New York: Syracuse University, June 1977.

————. "Urban Public Finances in Developing Countries: A Case Study of Metropolitan Ahmedabad." Urban and Regional Report No. 77-4. August 1975.

Bahl, Roy W.; Brigg, Pamela; and Smith, Roger S. "Urban Public Finances in Developing Countries: A Case Study of Metropolitan Manila." Urban and Regional Report No. 77-8. April 1976.

Bahl, Roy W., and Wasylenko, Michael J. "Urban Finances in Seoul." *Development Digest* 14 (April 1976):20–30.

————. "Urban Public Finances in Developing Countries: A Case Study of Seoul, Korea." Urban and Regional Report No. 77-3. April 1976.

Bougeon-Maassen, Francine. "Urban Public Finances in Developing Countries: A Case Study of Metropolitan Bombay." Urban and Regional Report No. 76-13. August 1976.

Bougeon-Maassen, Francine, and Linn, Johannes F. "Urban Public Finances in Developing Countries: A Case Study of Metropolitan Kingston, Jamaica." Urban and Regional Report No. 77-7. August 1975.

Doebele, William A.; Grimes, Orville F., Jr.; and Linn, Johannes F. "Participation of Beneficiaries in Financing Urban Services: Valorization Charges in Bogota, Colombia." *Land Economics* 55 (February 1979):73–92. Also World Bank Reprint Series: Number 99.

Linn, Johannes F. "Automotive Taxation in the Cities of Developing Countries." *Nagarlok Urban Affairs Quarterly* (India) XI (January–March 1979):1–23.

————. "The Distributive Effects of Local Government Finances in Colombia: A Review of the Evidence." In R. Albert Berry and Ronald Soligo (eds.), *Economic Policy and Income Distribution in Colombia.* Boulder, Colorado: Westview Press, 1980. Also World Bank Staff Working Paper No. 235. March 1976.

————. "Property Taxation in Bogota, Colombia: An Analysis of Poor Revenue Performance." *Public Finance Quarterly* 8 (October 1980):457–476.

————. "Public Utilities in Metropolitan Bogota: Organization, Service Levels, and Financing." Urban and Regional Report No. 78-2. May 1976.

————. "Urban Finances in Developing Countries." In Roy Bahl (ed.), *Urban Government Finance Emerging Trends.* Beverly Hills: Sage Publications, 1981.

————. "Urban Public Finances in Developing Countries: A Case Study of Cartagena, Colombia." Urban and Regional Report No. 77-1. January 1975. ˙

Linn, Johannes F.; Lethbridge, Nicholas; and Whitehead, Stuart. "Urban Public Finance in Project Preparation: An Operational Approach." *United Malayan Banking Corporation Economic Review* XIV (1978):66–82.

Linn, Johannes F.; Smith, R.S.; and Wignjowijoto, H. "Urban Public Finances in Developing Countries: A Case Study of Jakarta, Indonesia." Urban and Regional Report No. 80-7. May 1976.

Prud'homme, Rémy. "Urban Public Finances in Developing Countries: A Case Study of Metropolitan Tunis." Urban and Regional Report No. 77-2. January 1975.

Strategic Planning to Accommodate Rapid Growth in Cities of Developing Countries ("The City Study")

Ref. No. 671-47

In the past few decades, many large cities in developing countries have experienced extremely high population growth, which has created the need for massive public investment and the expansion of public services. In response, the World Bank has increased its share of lending for projects in urban areas and attempted to target benefits of projects on low-income segments of the urban population. Designing projects and programs that provide more urban infrastructure and serve the needs of the poor has strained available knowledge about how cities in less developed countries function. Projects are typically analyzed on a sectoral basis, and relatively little is known about their impacts on development within a city, including residential and employment location, travel patterns, and demand for public services.

The study's principal objectives are to analyze the determinants of urban development patterns, the effects of urban projects on these patterns, and their effect on the welfare of urban households. The study will test the applicability of existing techniques and develop new tools to estimate the spatial and economic impact of policy interventions, including the planning, execution, and evaluation of projects.

Urban phenomena are difficult to analyze, chiefly because many aspects of the urban economy are interrelated. For example, changes in employment location will affect housing markets, employment opportunities, transport flows, and the need for public services. At the same time, each aspect has an identity and an analytical basis of its own that permits a separate examination. In this study, five such components of the urban economy are identified: housing, transportation, employment location, labor force, and local public finance.

Within each of the five categories, three major research tasks are being carried out. First, the study is providing, to the extent permitted by the data, a systematic description of the current state and recent changes in the economy of a city and its spatial patterns. Second, it is producing estimates of behavioral parameters, such as price and income elasticities of demand, that will be useful as inputs to simple determinations of the impact of policies. Finally, these parameter estimates are being incorporated in analytical procedures, such as small sectoral and cross-sectoral models that can be used to carry out hypothetical analyses of the effect of a certain policy. The analytical tools and models are expected to prove useful to the staff of the Bank in the design and implementation of projects in urban areas, as well as to planning officials and decision makers in the developing countries.

The proposed research is being carried out in the form of a case study of Bogota, Colombia. Portions of the study are being extended to the city of Cali, in order to test the transferability of the parameter estimates and behavioral relations. The basic data sources for the project are the national population and economic censuses, various sample surveys of the 1972 Phase II Bogota Urban Development Study, a 1978 household survey, a survey of industrial establishments, and case studies of several *barrios*.

The data collection and descriptive phases of the project are complete, as is nearly all of the work on the estimation of behavioral parameters and the development of analytic tools. Numerous papers are available in the Urban and Regional Economics Division's Urban and Regional Report series, in the Working Paper series of the Corporación Centro Regional de Población in Bogota, and in other publications. The final output of the project will be contained in a series of six research monographs that will be produced in the coming year.

Responsibility: Development Economics Department—Gregory K. Ingram, Andrew M. Hamer, Kyu Sik Lee, Johannes F. Linn, Rakesh Mohan, Alvaro Pachon, and Richard B. Westin have been working on the project. Corporación Centro Regional de Población (CCRP) in Bogota is the project's main collaborating institution, and the CCRP staff members principally involved include Ramiro Cardona, José Fernando Piñeda, and Rodrigo Villamizar. The Chamber of Commerce of Bogota has been actively involved in disseminating the project's results and is now supporting additional analysis in Bogota. The Urban and Regional Development Section of the Colombian National Planning Office has provided general assistance. In Cali, the Departmental and Municipal Planning Office has participated directly in the project.

Completion date: July 1982.

Reports:

Carroll, A. "Pirate Subdivisions and the Supply of Residential Lots in Bogota." World Bank Staff Working Paper No. 435. October 1980.

Cifuentes J., and Hernandez, A. "Urban Transportation in Bogota." Urban and Regional Report No. 79-7. June 1978.

Fields, G. "How Segmented is the Bogota Labor Market?" World Bank Staff Working Paper No. 434. October 1980.

Ingram, G.K. "Housing Demand in the Developing Metropolis:

Estimates from Bogota and Cali, Colombia." Urban and Regional Report No. 81-11. April 1981.

————. "Land in Perspective: Its Role in the Structure of Cities." In M. Cullen (ed.), *Proceedings of World Congress on Land Policy.* Lexington, Massachussetts: D.C. Heath, 1981. Also Urban and Regional Report No. 80-9. November 1980.

Ingram, G.K., and Carroll, A. "The Spatial Structure of Latin American Cities." *Journal of Urban Economics* 2 (March 1981).

Latorre, E. "TASSIM-Cali: El Modelo de Demanda de Transporte para Cali." Documento de Trabajo No. 10. Bogota: Corporación Centro Regional de Población, July 1980.

Lee, K.S. "Determinants of Intra-Urban Location of Manufacturing Employment: An Analysis of Survey Results for Bogota, Colombia." Urban and Regional Report No. 81-3. March 1981.

————. "Intra-Urban Location of Manufacturing Employment in Colombia." In *Journal of Urban Economics* 2 (March 1981).

————. "A Model of Intra-Urban Employment Location: An Application to Bogota, Colombia." In *Journal of Urban Economics* (forthcoming, 1982).

Lee, Y.J. "The City Study: The Available Data, Vol. II." Urban and Regional Report No. 79-13. August 1979.

————. "The Spatial Development of Brazil Metropolitan Areas." Urban and Regional Report No. 81-12. July 1981.

Mohan, R. "The Determinants of Labor Earnings in Developing Metropoli: Estimates from Bogota and Cali, Colombia." Urban and Regional Report No. 80-14. November 1980.

————. "The People of Bogota: Who They Are, What They Earn, Where They Live." World Bank Staff Working Paper No. 390. May 1980.

Mohan, R.; Garcia, J.; and Wagner, W. "Measuring Malnutrition and Poverty: A Case Study of Bogota and Cali, Colombia." World Bank Staff Working Paper No. 447. April 1981.

Mohan, R., and Hartline, N. "The Poor of Bogota: Who They Are, What They Do, and Where They Live." Urban and Regional Report No. 80-6. July 1980.

Mohan, R., and Villamizar, R. "The Evolution of Land Values and Urban Structure in the Context of Rapid Urban Growth: A Case Study of Bogota and Cali, Colombia." In M. Cullen, (ed.), *Proceedings of World Congress on Land Policy.* Lexington, Massachussetts: D.C. Heath, 1981. Also Urban and Regional Report No. 80-10. October 1980.

Pachon, A. "Household Transportation Decisions in the Developing Metropolis." Paper presented at Latin American Meetings of the Econometric Society, Rio de Janeiro, Brazil, July 1981.

Piñeda, J.F. "Residential Location Decisions of Multiple Worker Households in Bogota, Colombia." Paper presented at Eastern Economic Association Meetings, Philadelphia, Pennsylvania, April 1981.

Reyes, L. "El Area Metropolitana de Cali." Documento de Trabajo No. 3. Bogota: Corporación Centro Regional de Población, May 1980.

Stevenson, R. "Housing Programs and Policies in Bogota." Urban and Regional Report No. 79–8. June 1978.

Valverde, N. "The City Study: The Available Data, Vol. I." Urban and Regional Report No. 79–6. June 1978.

Villamizar, R. "The Behavior of Land Prices: Its Determinants and Effects on Urban Structure." Paper presented at Latin American Meetings of the Econometric Society, Rio de Janeiro, Brazil, July 1981.

_____. "Land Prices in Bogota Between 1955 and 1978." In V. Henderson (ed.), *Research in Urban Economics, Vol. 2.* Greenwich, Connecticut: JAI Press, 1981. Also Urban and Regional Report No. 80–2. April 1980.

Wiesner, G. "Cien Años de Desarrollo Histórico de los Precios de la Tierra en Bogotá." Documento de Trabajo No. 4. Bogotá: Corporación Centro Regional de Población, May 1980.

The Urban and Regional Reports are available from the Urban and Regional Economics Division, Development Economics Department. Several papers are also available in the working paper series of the Corporación Centro Regional de Población, Bogota, Colombia.

National Spatial Policies: Brazil and Korea

Ref. No. 672-13

Policy makers in various countries are concerned about the degree to which population and economic activity is concentrated in a few urban centers. Many countries have experience with policies aimed at deconcentrating such activity. In the process, governments, as well as the Bank's operational staff, have become aware that substantive conceptual and empirical work on this subject is lacking, especially as it relates to developing countries. This research project is the first in a program aimed at responding to some of the more important of these concerns.

The project focuses on spatial issues in Brazil, in particular those related to the patterns of urban and industrial growth in Greater Sao Paulo and its regional hinterland. Further case studies are anticipated; preparatory work on the Republic of Korea has taken place in 1981 and is expected to lead to a second study. A program is also being developed with collaborating institutions in India.

The project in Brazil has three major aspects. The first includes a review of the state of the art in the economics of systems of cities, leading to the development of a framework for an international comparison of patterns of urban concentration. It indicates the extent to which economic analysis can explain the varying conditions found worldwide in urban development. This framework contributes to a general review of spatial development and policies in Brazil and provides the foundation for an econometric model to be tested with data gathered from cities in southern Brazil. The first set of tasks also includes a series of background studies on demographic and industrial changes in Greater Sao Paulo and its hinterland that complement the cited econometric work and provide useful background for the other components of the project. In particular, work is under way on examining the degree to which the process of concentrated population growth has begun to experience a reversal. In addition, one study decomposes the pattern of industrial growth into expansion by stationary firms and by firms that must make explicit choices about new locations. The findings about the latter will provide some indications of the potential impact of policy interventions on the spatial distribution of economic activity.

The second and major component of the study is an analysis of the determinants of the behavior of industrial firms in deciding where to locate. This includes an attempt to identify the effects that different types of spatial policy instruments have on the location of enterprises. An extensive survey of 600 new branch plants and independent firms in Sao Paulo State provides the principal data for this exercise. This will be complemented, where possible, by analyses of other existing surveys. The set of communities where surveyed firms are located has been studied. These areas differ in size and are at varying distances from metropolitan Sao Paulo. Using secondary data, an attempt has been made to determine the degree to which the level of urban services varies over space. This examination will serve to place the responses of surveyed firms about the adequacy of services at the municipal level in context. Some effort is also being made to understand the behavior of factor markets that condition the responses found in the survey. Aside from gathering information on land and freight costs at different distances from Greater Sao Paulo, analysis is under way on the spatial variation of wages.

The effectiveness of national spatial policies is often reduced by nonspatial public sector policies, which have spatial biases embedded within them. The project's third component, therefore, traces the spatial impact of selected nonspatial policies in Brazil, concentrating primarily on industrial sector programs (trade, fiscal incentives, credit subsidies) and on intergovernmental relations. In particular, the net protection afforded to different industrial sectors by the public sector's tariff, fiscal, and credit policies is being calculated. Through an analysis of the regional distribution of each output of each industrial sector, the value of implicit subsidies to different regions will be determined.

Data limitations and budgetary constraints do not permit empirical analyses of the adjustments that may be expected in the location of economic activity resulting from changes in the present set of policies in the public sector. Such adjustments can, however, be traced through analytically, by adapting models from international trade theory. The spatial implications of Brazil's system of intergovernmental relations, particularly those relating to tax and expenditure policies at the federal, state, and municipal level, are being examined. In both sets of tasks, an effort has been made to review the impact of such policies on the relations between major agglomerations in southern Brazil, especially metropolitan Sao Paulo, and the hinterland extending over a radial distance of several hundred miles. An important concern at this point is whether public sector policies tend to promote or hinder any process of deconcentration that might take place, whether spontaneous or induced by specific spatial incentives.

Responsibility: Development Economics Department—The Brazil study is managed by Andrew M. Hamer, in collaboration with William Dillinger, Eric Hansen, and David J. Keen. Vernon Henderson, Frances Ruane, Peter Townroe, and William Tyler are consultants.

Secondary data are being gathered and analyzed primarily with the aid of the Fundação Instituto Brasileiro de Geografia e Estatistica. The analyses of the impact of the public sector on cities of different sizes relies on the collaboration of the National Planning Secretariat, through its Instituto de Planejamento Económico e Social. Work on the component on industrial location is being conducted jointly with the Fundação Instituto de Pesquisas Económicas of the University of Sao Paulo.

Completion date: June 1982.

Reports

The following papers are available:

Henderson, J. Vernon. "A Framework for International Comparisons of Systems of Cities." Urban and Regional Report No. 80-3. March 1980.

Meyer, John R. "Report on Proposed Korea Spatial Study." Urban and Regional Report No. 81-1. March 1981.

Song, B.N., and Choe, S.C. "Review of Urban Trends and Policies in Korea." Urban and Regional Report No. 81-2. May 1981.

Townroe, P. "A Framework for the Study of New Industrial Decentralization from Metropolitan Sao Paulo, Brazil." Urban and Regional Report No. 81-8. May 1981.

"Coding Manual and Simple Frequency Distributions of the 1980 Sao Paulo Industrial Location Survey." Urban and Regional Report No. 81-9. May 1981.

Identifying the Urban Poor: A Case Study of Brazil

Ref. No. 672-37

A basic objective of the World Bank's project lending is to transfer benefits as directly as possible to the poor. In middle-income countries, "target groups" for projects are identified on the basis of relative poverty: one-third of the national income per head—adjusted for price differences between rural and urban areas—gives an income threshold below which an individual is considered poor.

Difficulties are frequently encountered in using this income threshold to identify the poor for the Bank's operations. First, the use of an indicator of individual income can be misleading, since most people live in family groups and what defines poverty is the income available to be shared among the household members. Second, a household poverty threshold, if it can be established, must be converted into units that are commonly used in local statistical tabulations. Third, especially in large countries, geographical variations in income and price levels may seriously compromise the use of a single, national, indicator of poverty. Finally, where rapid inflation is not offset by adjustments in wage levels, indicative income levels may quickly become outdated.

For lending projects in Brazil, the urban poverty threshold has been defined as equivalent to a family income of three minimum salaries. The minimum salary is defined by law and regionally differentiated; it is the unit used in most Brazilian income statistics. This threshold is used on a national basis. However, if the regional minimum salaries do not adequately reflect regional price differences, the living standard represented by three minimum salaries may vary substantially between regions. It is also possible that very few people in, say, Curitiba, live in the kind of poverty found in, say, Sao Luis, even though the Bank's urban poverty threshold discriminates many families in both cities as below the poverty line. As a result of these uncertainties, the Bank may be misdirecting its efforts against urban poverty and/ or making erroneous claims about the success of these efforts.

The Latin America and the Caribbean Projects Department has begun a study to investigate the degree to which the use of a single urban poverty threshold in Brazil may bias the design and evaluation of projects. This study will examine a set of indicators of the quality of life represented by three minimum salaries: for example, food consumption, type of housing, education, and mortality rates. If differences are detected, the research will investigate the potential of (1) regionally based income thresholds of the same type and (2) other possible indicators of poverty. The study will also develop procedures for regularly updating the poverty indicators, if this is found necessary.

Though the study will be carried out in Brazil, the method to be developed will be generally applicable in countries that have regional variations in prices and incomes. The results of the study should make it easier to design and evaluate projects to reach the urban poor, and also reduce the costs of collecting and using data on urban poverty.

Responsibility: Latin America and the Caribbean Projects Department—Peter L. Watson. The study is being carried out by James Hicks and David Velter of PLANPUR, a consulting firm based in Rio de Janeiro. The draft final report is under revision.

Completion date: December 1981.

Housing Demand and Housing Finance in Developing Countries (Phase I)

Ref. No. 672-46

Housing-related projects have constituted an important component of the World Bank's urban lending program during the past decade. This study is intended to shift the focus of research on housing from issues connected with project planning to those at the sectoral level, in consonance with a similar shift in the lending program.

The proposed work plan consists of three closely related clusters of analysis, all of which build upon existing work—"Analyzing the Effects of Urban Housing Policy in Developing Countries" (Ref. No. 671–37), now completed, and "The City Study" (Ref. No. 671–47 in this category). The first two clusters constitute Phase I of the program, which began in July 1981. The first cluster involves an extension of studies of housing demand to data sets from several developing countries. It is intended to examine whether a similarity in demand parameters indicated by recent evidence gathered in Colombia, El Salvador, and the Republic of Korea, holds across a broader range of developing countries and, if not, whether the differences can be explained. A second objective is to obtain a clear idea of the magnitude of the relevant parameters, which will be useful both at the project and sector level. In the project context, for example, demand parameters are used in decisions about the affordability of a project for target groups of households; in the sector context, they are used to evaluate the impact of market interventions such as tax changes on the availability of finance for housing.

The second cluster of analysis concentrates on the demand for particular attributes of the housing bundle such as lot size, the level of public services, or dwelling type. The work will focus especially on those attributes that are essentially fixed at the design stage of a housing development and are subsequently difficult to modify. This will help in minimizing misjudgments concerning such attributes, which can be particularly costly. Although parameter estimates will be compared cross-nationally, work on the second cluster will cover fewer countries than on the first, because of data limitations.   ·

Data needs of Phase I will be met by household level surveys of samples selected at random from the relevant urban populations. The surveys cover socioeconomic characteristics of the households, including household size, age, sex, occupations and monthly incomes of household members, and ownership of the dwelling units; as well as characteristics of the dwelling units, such as size, number of rooms, materials used, utilities, location, value of the unit, and rent paid. Existing data sets will be used to the extent possible. A preliminary list of countries includes Brazil, Colombia, Arab Republic of Egypt, India, Kenya, Republic of Korea, and the Philippines.

As tentatively planned, Phase II of the project will examine how the availability of housing finance affects a household's choice of tenure (renting, owning, squatting) and its consumption of housing. Issues of particular concern for the econometric work include the relation between financing and homeownership rates in cities, the relation between financing and levels of housing consumption, and the interaction between housing finance and price increases in housing markets. This phase is scheduled to be submitted for approval during the winter of 1982/83.

The methods to be adapted and developed for use in this project will be refined and simplified for use in operational work. In addition, the conceptual and methodological advances on tenure choice and finance will be useful in guiding urban sector work.

Responsibility: Development Economics Department—Douglas H. Keare, Stephen Mayo, and Michael Bamberger. James Follain of Syracuse University and Emmanuel Jimenez of the University of Western Ontario are principal consultants to the research project.

Completion date: April 1983.

8

Population and Human Resources

8–A. Education

Education and Rural Development in Nepal and Thailand

Ref. No. 671–49

The formal schooling level of farmers is correlated with their efficiency as farm managers, and exposure of farmers to extension education improves agricultural efficiency. There are also indications that the formal schooling level of rural women is often correlated with the number of children they bear. Changes in agricultural productivity and population growth are two important dimensions of rural development. To the extent that education and adult information services do influence these variables, alternative governmental education policies may affect the course of rural development.

The existing literature leaves two important questions unanswered. The first is: "To what extent do the observed correlations result not from the effects of education, but from attributes of individuals correlated with, but not caused by, their having received education?" The second, closely related, question is: "Through which of their outcomes do schooling and extension have whatever effects they do have?" This study explores these relationships by designing appropriate survey instruments, conducting surveys in Nepal and Thailand, and drawing conclusions from the resulting data.

Survey instruments were designed to obtain two categories of data that were previously unavailable. The first assesses data on the family background of the head of the farm household and that person's spouse. The second measures the ability, academic achievement, and modernity of attitudes of adult members of the households surveyed. Both sets of data are being used to ascertain the extent to which the apparent contribution of education to productivity results not from education itself, but rather from such correlates of education as ability or family background. Results from the tests are being used to quantify the contribution of each of education's measured outcomes to an increase in productivity and a decline in fertility.

Inclusion in the sample of villages exposed to reformed extension services and unexposed villages with similar populations and agricultural conditions allows a quantitative assessment of the benefits of extension. Data on farmers' agricultural knowledge and practices are permitting analysis of the mechanisms through which extension education is having its effects.

The basic tools for analyzing the effects of extension and formal education on agricultural productivity are production, profit, and factor demand functions. The magnitude and significance of the coefficients of the various education variables in these functions are the principal measures of their impact.

The detailed income data contained in these two data sets permit the determination of education's relationship to fertility, taking account of income. In addition, it is possible to show how education influences the biological determinants of the number of children (e.g., through improving maternal and child health and nutrition, or raising the age of marriage), as well as both husbands' and wives' demand for children. In Nepal, more emphasis is being placed on the biological supply of children than on the demand, since evidence indicates that actual fertility is constrained by biological factors. In Thailand, equal emphasis is being given to supply and demand. In Nepal, data have been gathered on the health and nutritional status of young children in the households sampled, allowing examination of the effect of their parents' education on these variables.

Responsibility: Development Economics Department—Dean T. Jamison and Susan H. Cochrane, in collaboration with Bal Gopal Baidya, Nirmala Joshi, Lawrence J. Lau, Pichit Lertamrab, Joanne Leslie, Marlaine Lockheed, Peter Moock, François Orivel, Rajendra Shrestha, Manu Seetisarn, and other consultants.

Completion date: December 1981.

Reports:

Baidya, B.G.; Chow, E.C.; Jamison, D.T.; Moock, P.R.; and
Shrestha, R. "Evaluating the Impact of Communications on

Agricultural Development: General Observations and a Case Study from Nepal." Paper presented at the Workshop on the Economics of Communications, East-West Communication Institute, Honolulu, June 1980. Forthcoming in M. Jussawalla and D. Lamberton (eds.), *Economics of Communication*. London: Pergamon Press, 1981.

Cochrane, S.H. "Determinants of Fertility and Child Survival in the Nepal Terai." World Bank: Development Economics Department, 1981.

Cochrane, S.H.; Joshi, N.; and Nandwani, K. "Fertility Attitudes and Behavior in the Terai." World Bank: Development Economics Department, 1980.

Jamison, D.T.; Baidya, B.G.; and Leslie, J. "Determinants of the Literacy and Numeracy of Adults in the Terai Region of Nepal." Paper presented at the Eastern Economic Association Meetings, Boston, Massachusetts, May 1979.

Jamison, D.T., and Moock, P.R. "Farmer Education and Farm Efficiency in Nepal: The Role of Schooling, Cognitive Skills, and Extension Services." World Bank: Development Economics Department, 1981.

Leslie, J.; Baidya, B.G.; and Nandwani, K. "Prevalence and Correlates of Childhood Malnutrition and Diarrheal Disease." World Bank: Development Economics Department, 1981.

Leslie, J., and Jamison, D.T. "Maternal Ability and Child Malnutrition in Nepal." World Bank: Development Economics Department, 1978.

Lockheed, M.E., and Jamison, D.T. "Some Determinants of School Participation in the Terai Region of Nepal." World Bank: Development Economics Department, 1979.

Economics of Educational Radio

Ref. No. 671-54

In 1975, the World Bank's Education Department began a review of experience with educational radio. This review, the results of which were published in 1977, generated several conclusions relevant to educational lending policy for the Bank:

1. Radio can be used, if programmed with care, to improve the quality of instruction at the elementary level.
2. Radio, combined with correspondence materials and occasional face-to-face instruction, can be a low-cost alternative

to traditional means of providing secondary and higher education. Used in this way for "distance teaching," radio appears capable of educating hitherto excluded groups.

3. Few instances appear to exist where educational television is superior to radio.

That study also identified two areas in which additional research would be beneficial. The first was research on the economics of radio for distance teaching. Despite a widespread impression that distance teaching is much less expensive than traditional instruction, little empirical information exists on its cost and cost effectiveness. The second area identified was the impact of in-school radio on student dropout and repetition rates. If radio resulted in even a modest reduction in repetition rates, it could more than pay for itself through reducing costs.

The present research centers around the potential of educational radio in its two most promising uses: distance teaching and the improvement of quality in schools. The study of the economics of radio for distance teaching provided information on costs and effectiveness of distance teaching for a wide range of experience: the preparation of adults for equivalency examinations at the beginning secondary level in Brazil, university instruction in Israel, teacher training in Kenya, and secondary education in the Republic of Korea, Malawi, and Mauritius. The purpose of distance teaching systems is remarkably constant from country to country. These systems are principally designed to extend the access to formal education to groups of people who were excluded from traditional schooling, either geographically or because of the need to maintain jobs during school hours in order to support themselves. A related purpose of distance teaching systems is to reduce the cost of providing instruction. Because of the apparently well-established potential of distance teaching simultaneously to improve equity and reduce costs, provision of substantial amounts of new information on the cost effectiveness of distance learning systems was viewed as useful. The distance-teaching study was substantially completed in 1978 and a supplementary case study on Brazil was finished in February 1980.

A second aspect of the project is an in-depth examination of the cost effectiveness of the Nicaragua Radio Mathematics Project. Statistical determinants and economic consequences of changes in dropout and repetition rates, with particular emphasis on the impact of introducing radio, are being examined.

This research will be useful in two important ways. Its principal purpose is to assist in the formulation of the World Bank's education projects. The information that this research will generate is designed to provide answers to remaining questions in project economics and to provide additional paradigms for use as project models. More generally, the project will substantially increase the quantitative knowledge of the impact of educational radio both in school and through distance teaching; as educational planners are increasingly turning to nontraditional options, this knowledge should be useful to them. In order to make the research results of maximal value outside the Bank, preliminary results were presented at a conference, sponsored by Unesco in June 1978, at the University of Dijon (France). This conference brought together educational planners and policy makers from all over the world to discuss the planning and economics of the use of electronic media for formal and nonformal education.

Responsibility: Education Department and *Development Economics Department*—Shigenari Futagami and Dean T. Jamison, respectively, in collaboration with David Hawkridge (United Kingdom), François Orivel (France), John Nkinyanji and Peter Kinyanjui (Kenya) for work on Kenya; João Oliveira and Mariza Oliveira (Brazil), François Orivel and Associação Brasileira de Teleducação for work on Brazil; Bernard Braithwaite (United Kingdom) and Korean Educational Development Institute for work on Korea; Arthur Melmed (United States), Uriel Turniansky and B. Ellenbogen (Israel), and Everyman University for work on Israel; Barbara Searle and Eduard George (United States) for work on Nicaragua; and Hilary Perraton and Anthony Bates (United Kingdom) for the overview. Unesco contributed to the travel expenses of these consultants.

Completion date: November 1981.

Reports

Batista, J., et al. *Telecurso Segundo Gran.* Rio de Janeiro: Associação Brasileira de Tecnologia Educacional, May 1980 (in Portuguese).

George, E. I. "Exploring the Effects of the Radio Mathematics Project on School-related Variables." In J. Friend, B. Searle, and P. Suppes (eds.), *Radio Mathematics in Nicaragua.* Stanford, California: Stanford University, Institute for Mathematical Studies in the Social Sciences, 1980.

Jamison, Dean. "Radio Education and Student Failure in Nicaragua: A Further Note." In J. Friend, B. Searle, and P. Suppes (eds.), Radio Mathematics in Nicaragua. Stanford: Stanford University, Institute for Mathematical Studies in the Social Sciences, 1980.

———. "Radio Education and Student Repetition in Nicaragua." In P. Suppes, B. Searle, and J. Friend (eds.), The Radio Mathematics Project: Nicaragua 1976–77. Stanford, California: Stanford University, Institute for Mathematical Studies in the Social Sciences, 1978. Also World Bank Reprint Series: Number 91.

Perraton, Hilary (ed.). Alternative Routes to Formal Education: Distance Teaching for School Equivalency. Baltimore and London: The Johns Hopkins University Press (forthcoming).

International Study of the Retention of Literacy and Numeracy

Ref. No. 671-55

This project is concerned with the measurement of the determinants of educational achievement and the relationship between acquired levels of skill and school leaving at the primary stage of education. Previous studies have suggested that the attenuation of literacy and numeracy skills among school leavers is a significant source of inefficiency in education systems. It has been suggested that there exist "threshhold" levels of learning beyond which retention of some skills is assured. However, such conclusions have usually been based on small, cross-sectional samples and the methods employed have ignored the linkage between in-school achievement and the decision by the child or the family to leave school. The purpose of this project is to test the so-called "educational wastage" hypothesis directly, using a longitudinal methodology that permits the joint determination of the acquisition of skills and the decision to drop out. Subsidiary purposes of the study are to measure the productivity of educational inputs from the home and from the school system, and to examine the consequences of the repetition of grades for achievement and school leaving. The results of the research are of fundamental interest to policy makers who, in the face of severe financial constraints and strong social pressure for schooling, are required to set and maintain minimum basic education requirements. Sponsorship of this research project reflects the high priority placed by the Bank, as well as by the Bellagio Group of donors, on basic education in developing countries.

The field work for the project is being carried out in the Arab Republic of Egypt. After completion of a pilot study in Cairo in 1977–78, a two-phase study was begun. Phase I was a nationwide cross-sectional study of 60 elementary schools. Two-thirds of the rural students and one-half of the urban students (8,370 students or 54 percent of the enrollment in grades 3–6) were tested to establish national norms of performance. Fifteen months later, 1,792 "dropouts" from the sample of 60 schools were traced and tested, using all the instruments applied to the in-school students.

Preliminary analysis of the cross-sectional sample revealed that a large proportion of the dropouts and some of the students from grades 3 and 4 were unable to achieve a positive score on the harder tests, whereas a few students from the higher grades received perfect scores. This led to a decision to model skill-specific achievement levels as censored normal variates. A general program for estimating censored and truncated regression functions was developed in August 1980. One of the consequences of modeling the censored distribution is that the differences in skill levels between grades are shown to be far larger than conventional analysis of variance models reveal.

In Phase II, a follow-up study retested the original dropouts, new dropouts, and one-third of the remaining students in school. The longitudinal study permits a more accurate assessment, at the level of the individual, of the influence of time on the erosion of basic skills. It also makes it possible to estimate the probability of dropping out at specific grade levels.

Data from the follow-up study have been used to revise the skill-specific achievement measures from the cross-sectional study. By classifying students who were in school in 1978–79 as either "continuing" or "leaving," it is possible to distinguish the skill levels of would-be school leavers from those of students continuing in school. Would-be dropouts are shown to have skill levels far closer to those of students already out of school than their continuing classmates. A plausible interpretation of these results is that "wastage" is caused not by the decision to drop out but by the failure of some students to acquire skills in school. At the present time, work is continuing on the development of a joint model of skill acquisition and the dropout decision.

The field work for the project has been conducted with the assistance of the National Centre for Educational Research (NCER) of the Ministry of Education in Cairo. NCER partici- pated in developing and testing survey instruments and was largely responsibile for planning and executing the field work. Assistance was also received from faculty members of the Uni- versity of Cairo, Ain-Shams University, and American University in Cairo.

Responsibility: Europe, Middle East, and North Africa Projects Department and Development Economics Department—Richard M. Durstine and Michael J. Hartley, respectively, in collaboration with Eric Swanson (consultant). Michael J. Wilson, at present Acting Chief, Education and Manpower Development Division, Europe, Middle East, and North Africa Projects Department, and Stephen P. Heyneman and Mulugueta Wodajo of the Education Department in the Central Projects Staff were actively involved in the initial stages of the project. In the Ministry of Education of Egypt, the responsible official is Dr. Youssef Khalil Youssef, Director, National Centre for Educational Research.

Completion date: The final report is scheduled for December 1981.

Reports

The papers listed below and other relevant papers are avail- able from the Education Department:

Kheiralla, Sayed. "An Inventory and Evaluation of Intelligence and Achievement Tests in Arabic Available in Egypt." December 1977.

Sheffield, James R. "Retention of Literacy and Basic Skills: A Review of the Literature." June 1977.

"The Completion Report" (including a Statistical Analysis of the Test and Interview Results). May 1978.

"The Retention of Basic Skills among School Leavers: A Prelimi- nary Report." Cairo: World Bank and NCER, February 1978.

"Socioeconomic and School Factors Influencing Success and Fail- ure in Elementary Schools in Egypt." Cairo: World Bank and NCER, March 1978.

"A Training Manual for Field Workers in the Literacy/Numer- acy Retention Project" (two parts). Cairo: World Bank and NCER, December 1978 and February 1979.

The following reports are available from the Technical Assistance and Special Studies Division of the Europe, Middle East, and North Africa Projects Department:

Hartley, M.J.; Poirier, D.J.; and Bencivenga, V. "A Statistical Methodology for the Egyptian Literacy Retention Study." 1979.

Hartley, M.J., and Swanson, E.V. "The Measurement of Learning and Retention Curves for Basic Skills in Egyptian Primary Education I: An Application of Censored Analysis of Variance." 1980.

Saad, S.L., with Makary, Khalil and N. "Dropout and Enrollment Statistics of the Sampled Schools." Cairo: National Centre for Educational Research, 1980.

Swanson, E.V., et al. "The Retention of Literacy/Numeracy Skills: An Overview for Basic Education in Egypt." 1981.

Textbook Availability and Educational Quality

Ref. No. 671-60

The quality of education in low-income countries is consistently low, contributing to the fact that, on average, school children from low-income countries appear to learn far less than do children in industrialized societies. The difference is believed to affect later technical and economic competence. Policy alternatives for improving the quality of education are few, and many proposals (such as reduction in class size) are costly and of dubious efficacy. But one approach that appears to be effective is to improve the availability of textbooks and reading materials.

The purpose of this research project is to attempt to replicate earlier findings of the effectiveness of textbooks, to obtain quantitative estimates of students' achievements in response to interventions that make textbooks available, and to extend the analysis of effectiveness studies to other variables, countries, and conditions.

In Phase I, completed in 1979, the 1972 Primary School Quality Project in Uganda had already provided a substantial number of lessons in the field of sociology and education. While this project, among others, showed that textbooks have an important influence on academic quality, this influence had not been isolated from other parallel influences within the classroom, such as teacher quality and physical facilities. The present research proj-

ect will make it possible to explore the independent influence of
textbooks and to weigh this influence against others with investment potential.

In Nicaragua, 40 randomly selected classrooms—20 in Grade 1
and 20 in Grade 4—have received funds to provide each child
with an up-to-date mathematics textbook. Conducted jointly by
the Institute for Mathematical Studies in the Social Sciences at
Stanford University and the Nicaraguan Ministry of Education,
the experiment has two purposes. The first purpose is to see
whether mathematics achievement can be increased by giving
each child a textbook and whether the increase is significantly
greater than the mathematics learned over the same period by a
randomly selected control group that is not receiving textbooks
through the experiment. The second purpose is to compare the
achievement gains of children who, in the same period, will be
exposed to mathematics by educational radio.

The World Bank's Third Education Project in the Philippines
provides for a large increase in the number of textbooks available
to children in public schools. As a result of this project, the average student-to-textbook ratio (in each school subject) will de-
crease from 10:1 to 2:1. The loan agreement stipulates that the
Government of the Philippines undertake an evaluation of the
project's impact. In addition, this evaluation includes funds to
provide additional texts to a small, randomly selected subsample
of primary schools, further to lower the student-to-textbook ratio
in the subsample from 2:1 to 1:1. The research project will assist
the Philippines' evaluation by bringing one of the individuals
responsible for the data collection to the World Bank, where the
data will be further analyzed and compared with data from
Uganda and elsewhere.

Significant quantities of information on educational quality
have been collected in the last few years and have not previously
been analyzed efficiently. In Phase II, approved by the Research
Committee in December 1978, the project has been analyzing
cross-section surveys of primary schools in Argentina, Bolivia,
Botswana, Brazil (Brasilia State only), Chile, Colombia, Arab Republic of Egypt, El Salvador, India, Iran, Mexico, Paraguay, Peru,
Thailand, and Uganda. The findings from these fifteen developing countries are then contrasted with results from similar primary school surveys conducted in fourteen industrialized nations.
Three questions are being asked of each data set: (1) which

school resources (including textbook availability) have, statistically, the greatest impact on academic achievement; (2) how equitable is the distribution of school resources; (3) do school resources in developing countries have more effect on academic achievement than they do in the United States and Western Europe, and do socioeconomic characteristics have less effect?

Responsibility: Education Department and *Development Economics Department*—Stephen P. Heyneman and Dean T. Jamison, respectively, in collaboration with William Loxley, Jorge Sanguinetty, Xenia Montenegro, and Ana-Maria Arriagada (consultants).

The organizations that have been collaborating in the sampling, instrument design, data collection, and analysis are: Regional Testing Centre, Gaborone, Botswana; Programa de Estudos Conjuntos de Integração Económica da America Latina (ECIEL), Rio de Janeiro, Brazil; National Centre for Educational Research, Cairo, Egypt; Oficina de Planeamiento y Organización (ODEPR), San Salvador, El Salvador; International Association for the Evaluation of Educational Achievement, Department of Comparative Education, University of Hamburg, Federal Republic of Germany; Education Projects Implementing Task Force (EDPITAF), Manila, Philippines; Institute of International Education, University of Stockholm, and International Association for the Evaluation of Educational Achievement, Department of Comparative Education, University of Stockholm, Stockholm, Sweden; National Institute of Education, Makerere University, Kampala, Uganda; Institute for Mathematical Studies in the Social Sciences, Stanford University, Stanford, California, and Program in Applied Labor Economics, American University, Washington, D.C., U.S.A.

Completion date: December 1981—Phase II.

Reports

Arriagada, Ana-Maria. "Determinants of Sixth Grade Student Achievement in Colombia." Mimeo. World Bank: Education Department, July 1981.

———. "Determinants of Sixth Grade Student Achievement in Peru." Mimeo. World Bank: Education Department, June 1981.

Galda, K.; Heyneman, S.P.; Jamison, D.T.; and Searle, B. "Improving Elementary Mathematics Education in Nicaragua: An

Experimental Study of the Impact of Textbooks and Radio on Achievement." In *Journal of Educational Psychology* (forthcoming).

Heyneman, S.P.; Farrell, J.P.; and Sepulveda-Stuardo, M. "Textbooks and Achievement: What We Know." World Bank Staff Working Paper No. 298 (also in Spanish and French). October 1978. Published in *The Journal of Curriculum Studies* 3 (1981):227–246.

Heyneman, S.P., and Jamison, D.T. "Student Learning in Uganda: Textbook Availability and Other Factors." In *Comparative Education Review* 24 (June 1980):206–220.

Heyneman, S.P., and Loxley, W. "The Distribution of School Quality Within High and Low Income Countries." Mimeo. World Bank: Education Department, September 1981.

_____. "The Impact of School Quality on Science Achievement Across 29 High and Low Income Countries." Paper presented at the Annual Meeting of the American Sociological Association, Toronto, Canada, August 1981.

_____. "The Influence of School Resources on Learning Outcomes in El Salvador." Paper presented at the Annual Meeting of the Comparative and International Education Society, Tallahassee, Florida, March 1981.

_____. "Influences on Academic Achievement Across High and Low Income Countries: A Re-Analysis of IEA Data." In *Sociology of Education* (January 1982).

Heyneman, S.P.; Loxley, W.; and Sanguinetty, J. *Codebook: School Achievement Survey for Brazil*. World Bank: Education Department, June 1981.

_____. *Codebook: School Achievement Survey for Six Spanish-Speaking Countries in Latin America* (available in English and Spanish). World Bank: Education Department, September 1980.

Heyneman, S.P., and Montenegro, X. "Home and School Factors Which Influence Student Learning in the Philippines." To appear as Chapter 6 in G. Feliciano and D. Jamison (eds.), *Improving School Quality in the Philippines: Evaluation Research and Educational Policy*. Manila: University of the Philippines Press (forthcoming).

Jamison, D.T., and Montenegro, X. "Evaluation of the Philippines Textbook Project: Multivariate Analysis of Data from Grades 1 and 2." To appear as Chapter 5 in G. Feliciano and

D. Jamison (eds.), *Improving School Quality in the Philippines: Evaluation Research and Educational Policy*. Manila: University of the Philippines Press (forthcoming).

Loxley, W. "The Effects of Schools on Learning in Egypt." Mimeo. World Bank: Education Department, September 1981.

_____. "The 'Husen Methodology' in the Context of School Effects Research Currently under Way in the Education Department." Mimeo. World Bank: Education Department, February 1980.

Education and Other Determinants of Farm Household Response to External Stimuli

Ref. No. 671–78

The objective of this study is to examine empirically the determinants of the quantitative response (changes in production, consumption, and, possibly, migratory behavior) of farm households to external stimuli. Data from a sample of individual farm households in Thailand, observed over a period of time, will be used. External stimuli include prices of farm outputs and inputs, wage rates, capital and land endowments, taxes, rents, availability of credit, irrigation, and size and composition of the household. The determinants that will be considered include degree of literacy; levels of education, nutrition, and health; availability and type of agricultural extension; proximity to markets; age, sex, religion, and other demographic and ethnic characteristics.

The basic framework is that of household utility maximization, although that assumption will be explicitly tested with the actual data. Previous studies conducted by the principal consultant suggest that the hypothesis of household utility maximization is consistent with actual data in a large number of developing countries.

A knowledge of the determinants of the quantitative responses of farm households in a developing country, or region within a country, can be extremely useful to economic and social policy makers. For example, predicting the response to an increase in the government support price of farm output may be important in deciding on the advisability of the price increase. The degree of response, however, may also depend on a complex of cultural, institutional, and societal factors, some of which can be controlled or influenced by a given policy. Thus, in order to assess

whether a price increase is desirable, one must consider the possible effects of accompanying policies that may change the
environment sufficiently to influence the characteristics of the
response. For example, whether a price increase has a positive
response may depend on the presence or absence of agricultural
extension work or on the level and distribution of education in a
locality.

The research project, therefore, proposes not only to study the
characteristics of the response of farm households to external
stimuli under static conditions, but also to investigate the way in
which the response characteristics may be modified as a result of
changes in the underlying environment. The end product will include an improved methodology for the construction of sectoral,
regional, or country models for the purpose of project appraisals
in agriculture. This project is using the data set on Thai farms
gathered under the research project "Education and Rural
Development in Nepal and Thailand" (Ref. No. 671-49 in this
category).

Responsibility: Development Economics Department—Dean T.
Jamison and Susan H. Cochrane. The principal researcher is Professor Lawrence J. Lau, Department of Economics, Stanford University, with the assistance of Erwin C. Chou (researcher).

Completion date: December 1981.

The Labor Market Consequences of Educational Expansion

Ref. No. 672-01

This research project is an evaluation of the massive investments in postprimary education made by developing countries
over the last several decades. The first phase consists of case
studies of Kenya and Tanzania. Sampling and survey methods to
generate data on adjustments in the labor market have been developed, as have various analytical tools to be applied to the data.
The study addresses such questions as:

1. Has educational expansion compressed the structure of earnings and reduced the inequality of pay?
2. Has educational expansion increased the productivity of
   wage labor?
3. Has expansion improved the distribution of educational opportunities and increased mobility between generations?

4. Has the expansion of postprimary education affected, through such mechanisms as migration and remittance flows, income levels and the distribution of income in regions from which migrants come to the large cities?

The principal analytical tool for the first part of the study is the wage function. An attempt will be made to assess the impact of a country's education and labor market policies on the structure of wages. For Kenya and Tanzania, simulation models will be estimated that will allow the use of counter-factual analysis to assess the efficacy of these policy regimes and to forecast the consequences of future educational expansion. The wage function analysis will then be coupled with aggregate measures of dispersion, in order to examine the effect of these policy regimes on the inequality of pay.

The second part of the study intends to rely mainly on the results of the ability and achievement tests administered to a subsample of the workers interviewed. Ability and years of schooling are the input, and cognitive skills the output, of education. By distinguishing the effects of these variables on wages, it will be possible to interpret the role that credentials, ability, screening, and human capital play in education.

The third portion of the analysis relies on information on the educational attainment of three generations: the worker, his parents, and his children. It is assumed that the children of the well-educated have a very high probability of gaining access to postprimary education and increasingly to postsecondary education as well. This implies that the access of children from lower socioeconomic groups to secondary and university education depends both on the size of these systems and on the demand they must meet from the well-to-do. It is hoped to establish how tight a relationship this is and to investigate whether there are policy steps that would make the mobility of lower socioeconomic groups less dependent on the rate of the overall expansion of education.

Since a very large proportion of urban workers are migrants from rural areas or smaller urban centers, the fourth part of the project will study the migration process, absorption into the urban labor force, and current socioeconomic ties with the areas where the migrants come from. Remittance functions can be estimated and other links analyzed to examine some of the effects of education beyond the larger urban centers.

The main source of information for this study is a specially designed survey of wage employees in randomly selected establishments. It is supplemented by other available sources of information on the labor market and the effects of education on earnings and their distribution. Interviews with employers are used to provide an understanding of their criteria for hiring and promotion of employees. Discussion with government officials are also conducted to inform the research.

These methods and tools developed in Eastern Africa are yielding answers to the four categories of questions cited above with a reasonable degree of statistical rigor. The answers, in turn, provide a basis for assessing the nature and magnitude of the benefits derived from the education investment programs of the countries concerned, and for establishing priorities for investing in education in the next decade.

Responsibility: Development Economics Department—Richard H. Sabot, in collaboration with A. Berry of the University of Toronto, A. Hazlewood and J. Knight of Oxford University (consultants), and J. Armitage and M. Boissiere of the Massachusetts Institute of Technology (researchers).

Completion date: June 1982.

Mass Media and Rural Development

Ref. No. 672-09

This project, which follows the research project "The Economics of Educational Radio" (Ref. No. 671-54 in this category), will undertake a study of the use of mass media for rural development. It will focus on two ways in which mass media have been used:

1. To supplement existing agricultural extension services, either through the upgrading of agents or by communicating directly to farmers.
2. To offer learning activities of various kinds to rural groups created for this purpose (e.g., farm forums, radio campaigns, radio listening groups, radiophonic schools).

While much education or information for rural adults is supplied face to face by the extension agents, the media are used increasingly as a supplement or even an alternative to this method. The research will review the available evidence on such projects and will summarize the literature in this field. In particular, the research will consider the benefits from these projects, including to what extent they contribute to women's development; assess what factors make them effective; and determine what their costs are relative to alternatives.

The provisional conclusions will be tested against field conditions by carrying out a limited number of case studies of rural education projects in Africa that Unesco has agreed to fund. The overview papers will be revised in the light of the data gathered in the case studies.

Responsibility: Education Department and *Development Economics Department*—Shigenari Futagami and Dean T. Jamison, respectively. Principal collaborators are Hilary Perraton and Lord Young of Dartington, both with the International Extension College in the United Kingdom.

Completion date: December 1981.

Diversified Secondary Curriculum Study

Ref. No. 672-45

Education authorities in a large number of developing countries have committed themselves, to some degree, to the diversification of curricula in secondary schools. Such diversification, in which practical and/or occupational subjects are introduced into an otherwise completely academic program, has been endorsed by the education community at large and is extensively supported by the Bank (it is a feature of half the education projects approved by the Bank in the last fifteen years). Its broad objective is to match the skills and aspirations of the majority of secondary school graduates more closely to the job opportunities open to them. There are two models of such diversification: one model introduces practical subjects as a component of a general curriculum with no direct occupational aims; the second introduces vocationally oriented subjects, with direct occupational aims, as subjects in which students may specialize.

Experience with curricular diversification reveals several recurrent problems, notably in the training of teachers of vocational subjects, the use and maintenance of facilities, and the attitudes of staff and students. More fundamental than these problems of implementation is evidence that conventional "academic" secondary education may have been dismissed too quickly—it may, in itself be an invaluable form of vocational training. There are also some more recent innovations in postprimary education and training that may be more cost-effective and otherwise more useful alternatives to traditional secondary education than the diversification of conventional curricula.

A study managed by the Bank's Education Department will test some of the assumptions that underlie diversification and evaluate the outcomes of practical/vocational curricula. It will be the first to undertake comprehensive and rigorous tests of the efficacy of diversification. The study will evaluate the effects of diversification according to the two models on the internal efficiency of schools (measured through tests of school graduates' cognitive abilities and attitudes) and external efficiency (measured in terms of school graduates' experience of unemployment and their job performance).

Case studies will be undertaken in two countries whose experience with diversified curricula is long enough to be evaluated meaningfully—Tanzania for the first model and Colombia for the second. To assess the effects of diversification on the internal and external efficiency of schools, the study will use cost-benefit analysis; data on earnings will be gathered from recent school graduates and leavers, and the analysis of costs will measure differences in the social cost between diversified and conventional schools. To supplement the quantitative analysis, existing and newly gathered data will be used to compare the broad features of diversified and conventional schooling, measured in terms of enrollments, dropout and graduation rates, and the post-secondary school choices made by school leavers.

The data to be collected will cover the costs of schooling under the two models; the socioeconomic background of students; the characteristics of communities, schools, and teachers; and the aspirations of students and their subsequent attainments. A subset of the graduates and school leavers to be studied will be traced after they have left school to assess how far their experiences differ according to the type of school they attended.

The conclusions to be drawn from the study as to the feasibility and effectiveness of diversification in different circumstances will, it is hoped, help to provide a policy framework for the Bank's further operations in secondary education and aid government decision making on curricula.

Responsibility: Education Department—George Psacharopoulos, *Latin America and the Caribbean Projects Department*—Ralph W. Harbison, and *Eastern Africa Projects Department*—Lawrence Wolff, in collaboration with the Colombian Ministry of Education and the Instituto SER de Investigación in Colombia and the Tanzanian Ministry of Education and Department of Education, University of Dar es Salaam, in Tanzania.

Completion date: July 1983.

8-B. Labor and Employment

Labor-Force Participation, Income, and Unemployment

Ref. No. 670-45

Improving the productivity of the urban poor requires knowledge of the operation of urban labor markets. Since recent migrants constitute a significant proportion of the growth in the urban labor force in many cities, such knowledge would also shed light on the impact that rural development policies have on different sectors.

Analysts have categorized the labor force into "formal" and "informal" sectors. This study examines both the linkages and contrasts between the two. The basic distinction hinges on the notion that employment in the "formal" sector is protected by barriers to entry imposed by trade unions and/or government, while the "informal" sector is characterized by a lack of firm contractual relationships, self-employment, and variable hours of work. This project emphasizes the study of employment and earnings in the "informal" sector of the labor market and the relationship among participation rates, individual earnings, and household income.

The major part of the research is devoted to a new survey of the labor market in Bombay (India). In Phase I, completed in April 1975, a survey of 1,000 casual workers was undertaken. Phase II, completed in June 1977, consisted of a survey of 2,500 workers from the "informal" sector and another 2,500 workers from the "formal" sector. Together, this body of data contains a wealth of information on the characteristics and incomes of the labor force found in the two sectors of the labor market and provides an opportunity for testing and modifying theories on urban labor markets proposed in the literature.

A part of the project was also devoted to an analysis of data obtained from an urban household survey in three towns in Malaysia. This part of the research, in addition to providing a point of contrast with Bombay, is complementary to a more comprehensive report, "Labor Market in Malaysia" (Ref. No. 670-43), a recently completed research project.

Responsibility: Development Economics Department—Dipak Mazumdar, in collaboration with the Economics Department of Bombay University for the survey work in that city.

Completion date: November 1981.

Reports

Mazumdar, Dipak. "Analysis of the Dual Labor Market in LDCs." In Subbiah Kanappan (ed.), *Studies of Urban Labor Market Behavior in Developing Areas.* Geneva: International Institute of Labor Studies, 1977.

———. "Labor Market Segmentation and the Determination of Earnings: A Case Study of Malaysia." World Bank Staff Working Paper No. 278. May 1978.

———. "Paradigms in the Study of the Labor Market in LDCs: A Reassessment in the light of an Empirical Survey in Bombay City." Paper presented at the Forty-eighth Annual Conference of the Southern Economic Association, Washington, D. C., November 1978. Also World Bank Staff Working Paper No. 366. December 1979.

———. "The Rural-Urban Wage Gap, Migration, and the Shadow Wage." *Oxford Economic Papers* 28 (November 1976):33–46. Also World Bank Reprint Series: Number Forty-two.

———. "The Theory of Urban Underemployment in Less Developed Countries." World Bank Staff Working Paper No. 198. February 1975. French translation in *L'Actualité française* (June 1977).

———. "The Urban Informal Sector." *World Development* (August 1976):665–679. Also World Bank Reprint Series: Number Forty-three.

———. *Urban Labor Markets and Income Distribution in Malaysia.* New York: Oxford University Press, 1980.

Employment Models and Projections

Ref. No. 671–06

Although a considerable amount of research is under way on labor force absorption and other aspects of employment in developing countries, a standard methodology for assessing trends in sectoral employment growth, factors contributing to these trends, and the future employment outlook has yet to emerge. This study's objective is to develop, apply, and evaluate such a methodology on the basis of case studies in India and Zambia. Monographs on field work in these countries will consist of:

1. An analysis of trends in sectoral employment and unemployment, supplemented by information on output growth, changes in capital intensity, demand mix, and factor prices.
2. A paper on the sources of employment growth, using input-output techniques to decompose sectoral employment growth into the relative and absolute contributions of final demand growth, changes in the final demand mix across sectors and expenditure categories, material input usage, and labor productivity.
3. A macroeconomic model of the economy.
4. A report on macroeconomic and employment projections that will estimate future labor absorption under alternative assumptions about investment, foreign exchange constraints, technical change, and the demand mix.
5. A policy statement derived from the foregoing that outlines feasible fiscal and other direct measures to influence the growth of final demand, the choice of technique, and the product mix so as to increase productive labor absorption.

Responsibility: Development Economics Department—Ardy Stoutjesdijk. The principal researcher is Raj Krishna of the Planning Commission, Government of India, in collaboration with Malcolm McPherson, Harvard University.

Completion date: The Zambia study has been completed. The completion date of the India study has not been determined.

Reports

Krishna, Raj. "Rural Unemployment: A Survey of Concepts and Estimates for India." World Bank Staff Working Paper No. 234. April 1976.

McPherson, Malcolm. "A Study of Employment in Zambia."
Available in manuscript form. World Bank: Development
Economics Department, May 1978.

Structure of Rural Employment, Income, and Labor Markets

Ref. No. 671-30

Agriculture and rural development projects assisted by the
World Bank are usually directed toward improving the lot of
farm households by a variety of means, ranging from the construction of irrigation facilities to the provision of subsidized inputs. Many households in rural areas, however, have no access to
land and are, therefore, not directly affected by such projects.
Others that have land must make production and consumption
decisions jointly. These family farms or agricultural households
combine two fundamental units of microeconomic analysis—the
household and the firm. Although traditional economic theory
has dealt with each separately, in developing agriculture domi-
nated by peasant family farms, it is their interdependence that is
of crucial importance. The purpose of the present research is to
quantify the extent to which the World Bank's agricultural projects could benefit landless or near-landless rural households that
depend on wage employment as their main source of income.
Also to be developed is a theory to integrate the firm (production) and household (consumption) aspects of decision making in
agricultural households that depend upon both wage employment
and farm production for their incomes.

The first phase of the research consisted of a critical review of
the large body of empirical studies on this topic that exist in
India and a comparative analysis of the impact of technological
change over time and space on labor demand and supply, and on
wage rates for selected areas in India. This phase of the research
is complete and two reports have been issued.

A second phase involved the analysis of multipurpose farm-
household data for the Republic of Korea. The objective was to
estimate household labor demand and supply curves in the context of a model that incorporates aspects of consumption and
production behavior in a theoretically consistent fashion. A theoretical model that integrates farm and household decisions in a
multicrop environment has been developed and its empirical esti-

mation has been completed. This work was done jointly with the Korea Rural Economics Institute, which provided detailed farm-household data for nearly 1,200 farms obtained from a nationwide survey. A report outlining the results and their implications for agricultural policies has been issued.

The final phase of the project applies the models developed earlier to a World Bank investment project being executed in Nigeria. The Northern Nigeria Agricultural Projects Monitoring, Evaluation, and Planning Unit (APMEPU) has completed a detailed household survey combining income, expenditure, and labor usage, based on weekly interviews over three years (1976–79) of a sample of about 800 households from the Gusau and Funtua project areas, where improved seed and extension services are being provided to approximately 80,000 households. The project is tied closely to the now-completed research project "Adoption of Farm Technology in Northern Nigeria" (Ref. No. 671–88). A model of short-run household behavior has been estimated to explain household consumption of both goods and leisure. This model serves as a means for predicting the response of household labor supply to different forms of project interventions. In addition, it allows the estimation of the impact of new production opportunities on household incomes and hence consumption, as well as the opposite impact of household choices between labor and leisure on farm production.

Finally, the research will attempt to assess the operation of the rural labor market in an attempt to determine how changes in the supply of family labor, as predicted by these household models, may be expected to affect wage employment and wage rates. In addition, the implications of integrating farm and household decisions in a unified model of the behavior of agricultural households will be examined.

Responsibility: Development Economics Department—Inderjit Singh. Kalpana Bardhan conducted the Indian phase of the project, and Professor Choong Yong Ahn of Choong Ang University, Republic of Korea, assisted with analysis of the Korean data. In addition, the Korea Rural Economics Institute cooperated in, and will continue the analysis of, the Korean data as subsequent surveys are completed and processed by it. The data for the Nigeria component of the study have been generated by the field evaluation unit established as part of the Gusau, Funtua, and Gombe Agricultural Projects in Nigeria. Janakiram Subramanian (consultant) assisted with the modeling and analysis. Professor Edi Karni from Tel Aviv University, Israel, assisted with the theoretical part of the model.

Completion date: The Indian and Korean components of the research project have been completed. The estimation of the Nigerian component has been completed and a report will be available in April 1982.

Reports

Ahn, C. Y.; Singh, Inderjit; and Squire, Lyn. "A Model of the Agricultural Household in a Multi-Crop Economy: The Case of Korea." Division Paper No. 58. August 1980. In *Review of Economics and Statistics* (forthcoming).

Bardhan, K. "Rural Employment and Wages and Labor Markets in India: A Survey of Research." Sections I, II, and III. *Economic and Political Weekly* XII, nos. 26, 27, and 28 (1977).

———. "Rural Employment and Wages with Agricultural Growth in India: Some Intertemporal and Cross-Section Analyses." Division Paper No. 38. March 1977.

Karni, Edi. "A Model of an Agricultural Household in a Multi-Crop Environment with Production Uncertainty." Division Paper No. 50. September 1979.

Singh, Inderjit, and Squire, Lyn. "A Model of the Agricultural Household: Some Implications for Nutrition Policies in Rural Areas." Division Paper No. 49. September 1978.

The Division Papers are available from the Employment and Rural Development Division, Development Economics Department.

Urban Labor Markets in Latin America

Ref. No. 671-48

This study of the structure of urban labor markets in Latin America arises from the World Bank's concern with the alleviation of urban poverty through raising the productivity of the employed labor force and expanding earnings opportunities. The study seeks a better understanding of the market and institutional determinants of the earnings structure and, thus, of the way in which economic growth is transmitted through the labor market. Related concerns of the study are the extent and causes of underutilized labor.

Earlier research on employment, including work done by the Bank, has been directed mostly at (1) analyzing the technological and factor market determinants of the demand for labor by the modern sector, particularly industrial establishments; (2) describing the personal and establishment characteristics of the urban informal sector; and (3) estimating earnings functions. This study seeks to complement earlier work by developing aggregate, yet detailed, statistics on labor market structure and flows and by examining the relationships between the urban modern and informal sector. The project will be useful to the Bank, first, as an illustrative model for country economic analysis of employment issues and, second, in a less direct way, by improving the understanding of urban labor market structure and behavior.

The research consists of case studies in two countries—Colombia and Peru—carried out in 1977. The principal tasks were the estimation of data on the flows of workers of different types into and through different types of employment; and the use of these data, as well as supply and demand analysis, to explain labor-market behavior over specific periods. Field work was based largely on existing data sources (censuses, household and establishment surveys, wage statistics, and available studies of particular labor market issues), supplemented by informal interviews of some establishments and workers.

The output of the study will consist of a report on each country, describing the findings on structure and behavior of urban labor markets, and a proposal for further work in this area.

Responsibility: Development Economics Department—Richard C. Webb, in collaboration with Albert Berry (consultant). Other consultants include Alison Scott of the University of Essex, United Kingdom, and a research team in Peru, consisting of Segundo Castro, Gabriela Villalobos, Marie Gabriela Vega, Tomas Malaga, and Carlos Eyzaguirre.

Completion date: November 1981.

Wage and Employment Trends and Structures in Developing Countries

Ref. No. 671-84

This project forms part of an evolving research program designed to provide a better foundation for analyses of change in wages and employment in individual countries; for the systematic compilation of comparable series on wages, employment, and other labor market phenomena (labor force participation, hours of work, skill formation, mobility); and for the development of analytical tools or models of the behavior of labor markets to appraise specific issues of employment and income policies.

Traditionally, the World Bank has been much concerned, particularly in the formulation of its lending programs and the preparation of its projects in developing countries, with allocative efficiency and hence with the relative rewards for different types of labor and their implications for labor efficiency. With the recent emphasis on problems of poverty alleviation and income distribution, attention has increasingly been focused both on the structure of relative wages and incomes, and on the rate at which the low-income work force can be employed in increasingly productive and remunerative activities.

At an operational level, these concerns with the efficiency and equity aspects of labor market phenomena need to be reflected in the design and evaluation of specific Bank projects and in the analyses and recommendations of the Bank's sector and country economic reports, as well as in broader development policy studies, such as the *World Development Report*. Moreover, some governments of developing countries are moving toward the use of wages and incomes policies to tackle distributional and poverty problems. The formulation and implementation of such policies presuppose a well-founded basis for explaining the determinants of existing wage structures and the means of controlling them.

In conceptualizing these concerns about wages, employment, incomes, and poverty, economists have developed various models to determine employment and wages that embody different implicit or explicit assumptions about the supply price of labor; about the wage determination process as part of the struture of the labor market; and about the effects of changing environmental (structural) characteristics of an economy on employment levels and real wages in different sectors. This research project is an effort to sort out the implicit assumptions underlying the differing views about how labor markets function (at both relatively aggregative and more micro levels) in developing countries, and to explore the usefulness of alternative broad sets of assumptions in the light of the evidence on the actual development experience in different countries.

The first component of the study reviewed the data currently collected to follow the labor market in developing countries, and examined the problems that varying conceptual and statistical characteristics pose for estimating time trends and making intercountry comparisons. In addition, the study sought a more comprehensive empirical assessment of aggregative trends in employment, unemployment, real wages, and labor incomes in developing countries, and explored comparative patterns and changes over time of wage and employment relationships between major economic sectors. This descriptive analysis updates and augments earlier inquiries into employment aspects of development, provides a basis for the formulation of certain "stylized facts" and tentative hypotheses about aggregative wage employment relationships, and will allow a better judgement about the areas were statistical improvements are most urgently needed.

In the second component, studies of the evolution of the labor market were undertaken in India, Kenya, and Mexico. The purpose of these studies is to analyze the relation of wage trends and structures to the experience of different types of developing countries and to the effects of government policy interventions on wages and incomes. Many past country studies of labor markets have concentrated on their most recent manifestations and on various projections into the future. In contrast, this project looks at the evolution of labor markets in the light of a longer period of development experience. (A fourth study on Brazil had to be cut short with the departure from the Bank of the principal researcher responsible, Richard Webb.) A special study on unemployment in India by Professor Raj Krishna of the Delhi School of Economics is analyzing trends in rural and urban unemployment of males and females over the period 1959–78, as well as variations in the incidence of unemployment across states in 1973 and 1979.

Responsibility: Development Economics Department—Mark W. Leiserson has overall responsibility for the project and Swadesh R. Bose is responsible for the aggregative cross-country component of the research. Peter Gregory is consultant for the Mexico study and Deepak Lal for the India and Kenya studies. All four researchers will also be involved in the development of the analytical and overall comparative aspects of the study. The Bureau of Statistics of the International Labour Office (ILO), Geneva, has collaborated in assembling and documenting time series on wages in major economic sectors in developing countries.

Other consultants and collaborators include: Professor Dharma Kumar and Dr. Bhaskar Dutta of the Delhi School of Economics and Professor Kanta Ahuja of the HCM State Institute of Public Administration, Jaipur, on the India study; Mr. Paul Collier, Oxford Institute of Statistics, on the Kenya study; Isaac Kerstenetzky, Instituto Brasileiro de Geografia e Estatistica (IBGE) on the Brazil study; Professor Peter Gregory, University of New Mexico, on the Mexico study; Professor Raj Krishna, Delhi School of Economics, on the study of unemployment in India.

Completion date: December 1981.

Reports

Bose, Swadesh. "Changes in Sectoral Wages in Developing Countries: Compilation of Data." Draft of a Division Paper. September 1980.

———. "Employment, Unemployment and Wages in Some African Countries: A Review of Evidence for Recent Decades." Draft of a Division Paper. May 1980.

———. "Trends in Employment, Unemployment and Wages in Developing Countries: A Review of Recent Decades." Draft of a Division Paper. November 1980.

Collier, Paul, and Lal, Deepak. "Coercion, Compassion and Competition: Wages and Employment Trends and Structures in Kenya 1800–1980." Division Paper No. 64.

Dutta, Bhaskar. "Industrial Wage Structures in India: A Survey." Division Paper No. 61. May 1980.

Gregory, Peter. "Economic Development and the Labour Market in Mexico." Division Paper No. 70. August 1981.

Kumar, Dharma, and Krishnamurthy, J. "The Evolution of Labour Markets in India, 1857–1947." Division Paper No. 72. May 1981.

Lal, Deepak. "Cultural Stability and Economic Stagnation: India 1500BC–1980—Wage and Employment Trends and Structures." Draft of a Division Paper. June 1981.

———. "Wages and Employment in the Philippines." Division Paper No. 57. October 1979.

Pfefferman, Guy Pierre, and Webb, Richard. "The Distribution of Income in Brazil." World Bank Staff Working Paper No. 356. September 1979.

Satyanarayana, Y. "Trends in Employment and Unemployment in India—An Analysis, Discussion and Compilation of Data." Draft of a Division Paper. August 1980.

————. "Wage Trends in India: 1830 to 1976—An Analysis, Discussion and Compilation of Data." Division Paper No. 74. August 1980.

The Division Papers are available from the Employment and Rural Development Division, Development Economics Department.

Structure of Employment and Sources of Income by Socioeconomic Groups and Regions in Peru

Ref. No. 672-40

In the face of unemployment amounting to over 7 percent of the labor force and falling real household incomes among the poor, Peru's government has attached a high priority to employment creation and antipoverty programs. However, this effort is hindered by a lack of basic knowledge of household behavior with regard to labor supply and income generation. The present research aims at filling this gap through a detailed study of the problem concentrating on the household as the unit of analysis. This approach has been adopted because, in the Peruvian context, it is the household that makes the decisions on how much to spend and how much to save—needs that determine the amount of income desired. The latter has a primary influence on decisions as to the number of household members entering the labor force under differing circumstances. The study is intended as a complement at the micro level to the Peru component of an earlier research project on "Urban Labor Markets in Latin America" (Ref. No. 671-48 in this category).

The data base is the ENCA survey (National Survey of Food Consumption) carried out in Peru in 1971-72. Cross-section analysis of this data will provide an insight into household behavior under conditions that vary widely, including those that prevail at present. Thus, the project is expected to produce detailed information on the working and income-generating behavior of Peruvian households, which would help in the design of income, employment, and education policies. The specific objectives of the research are (1) to identify factors underlying income differentials among workers such as education, age, and the number of working hours; (2) to examine household strategies aimed at earning a higher income, and worker's expectations as to future income according to type of occupation; (3) to determine levels of underemployment by estimating potential working hours from household units in each of the occupational categories analyzed; and (4) to determine regional income differences and the characteristics of the productive structure in each of the regions according to the degree of urbanization.

Responsibility: Latin America and the Caribbean Programs Department I and *Development Economics Department*—Ulrich R.W. Thumm and Constantino P. Lluch, respectively, in collaboration with the Research Center of the Pacific University (Centro de Investigación, Universidad del Pacífico).

Completion date: April 1982.

8–C. Population and Health

Population Growth and Rural Poverty

Ref. No. 671–02

High growth rates of population hinder the improvement of living standards in developing countries, especially among lower-income families. In many of the poorer countries, family planning programs have been adopted, but many of these have not yet succeeded in significantly reducing the rate of population increase. This situation requires further research on the determinants of fertility and the economic costs and benefits of larger families for rural households. Knowledge of this type may be of assistance in shaping policies other than family planning (e.g., for education, employment, social security), whose impact on fertility might be considered an explicit benefit.

The level of fertility in any society reflects ingrained and interrelated socioeconomic factors. The World Bank believes that these factors need to be analyzed in a variety of ways—by the study of fertility differentials at one point in time, by longitudinal assessment of the impact of development projects, and by a detailed study of small communities.

Under this research project, comparative anthropological studies of eight villages in India, Kenya, Nigeria, and Sri Lanka are being prepared. While each of the studies has its own distinct emphasis and focus, all have the common elements of considering the social and private forces that may affect fertility (e.g., the economic roles of children), the effects of rapid population growth on the local economy and social fabric, the perceptions held in the community about such change, and the reaction to it. A comparative overview of these common elements will be prepared by the project director.

Preliminary results were discussed at a mid-project conference held in December 1975. The papers, now published, include socioeconomic and demographic background studies on the villages and some initial findings on fertility patterns.

Responsibility: Development Economics Department—Timothy King. The study is directed by Professor Scarlett Epstein of the Institute of Development Studies, University of Sussex (United Kingdom). The field investigations have been carried out by eight graduate students from the selected countries who are currently attending the university, each of whom has spent more than a year in one of the villages. The Population Council and the Overseas Development Administration (United Kingdom) have joined the World Bank in financing this project.

Completion date: December 1981.

Reports

Epstein, Scarlett, and Jackson, Darrel (eds.). *The Feasibility of Fertility Planning: Micro Perspectives.* London: Pergamon Press, 1977.
_____. *Some Social Aspects of Population Growth: Cross-Country Studies.* Bombay: MacMillan, Ltd., 1975.

Narangwal Population and Nutrition

Ref. Nos. 671-38 and 672-03

The purpose of this study is to use household data, collected from 1966 to 1974 in Narangwal (Punjab), India, to analyze fertility, family planning, nutrition, health behavior, and the efficiency of service delivery systems. Within a controlled experimental design, groups of villages were provided with various combinations of health, family planning, and nutrition services, and households in each group were observed over time.

The analyses of the nutrition data explored the relative effects of poor nutrition and of other socioeconomic factors on the growth and development of preschool children. Determinants and associated factors of the demand for nutrition services were also studied.

Analysis of the population data addressed issues of policy significance, such as the influence of household socioeconomic and community characteristics on the utilization of health and family planning services, and the perception of child mortality on family planning acceptance, possible trade-offs between alternative levels of health and family planning services, and the relationship between contraceptive practices and fertility.

This analysis (Phase I), now completed, indicates that integration of family planning with health services was not only more effective than the provision of family planning in isolation, but was also efficient in terms of cost. Integration of these services produced better results in terms of the quality of contraceptive protection and a more equal distribution of services among various socioeconomic groups of users. Certain characteristics of the potential clients (e.g., education, communication with spouse) were found significant in predisposing them to accept contraception. The analysis has also identified a two-way relationship between the use of health services and the acceptance of family planning.

The health services added significantly to the acceptance of family planning. Experience in contraception before the program was a factor that facilitated acceptance of contraception during the program period and its contribution seemed to be greater in the case of health services initiated by the program than those by the client.

Although it may be anticipated that the full impact of a program of contraception on fertility will go beyond the life of the project, significant declines in fertility were observed. Births to acceptors covered by a program of family planning were substantially fewer than to nonacceptors.

Analysis (Phase II) of relationships over time between the practice of family planning, use of health services, and other predisposing characteristics is continuing. The main goal is to identify criteria for determining the most appropriate population groups and the best timing of efficient service combinations that will produce a specific cost-effective and/or equitable impact on the practice of family planning and on fertility. Narangwal research in Phase II, therefore, comprises the following tasks:

1. Input and output measures of the Narangwal services will be refined.
2. Further multivariate analyses will be done within experimental groups (across socioeconomic classes), as well as within a socioeconomic class across experimental groups.
3. Alternative hypothetical intervention strategies will be analyzed in a simulation framework to derive an optimal mix of service components for comprehensive health and family planning objectives.
4. Features of the Narangwal experiment that may be replicable in other Bank programs will be identified.

Responsibility: Development Economics Department—Rashid R. Faruqee. The collaborating research team from The John Hopkins University consists of Dr. Carl E. Taylor, Dr. R.S.S. Sarma, Dr. Robert L. Parker, and Dr. William A. Reinke.

Completion date: Phase I—October 1980; Phase II—December 1981.

Reports

The five studies listed below are available from the Development Economics Department:

Chernichovsky, D. "The Economic Theory of the Household and Impact of Measurement of Nutrition and Health Related Programs." World Bank Staff Working Paper No. 302. October 1978.

Faruqee, R. "Analyzing the Impact of Health Services: Narangwal and Other Experiences." Discussion Paper No. 81-6. March 1981.

Faruqee, R., and Johnson, E. "Health, Nutrition, and Family Planning: A Survey of Experiments and Special Projects in India." Discussion Paper No. 81-14. May 1981.

Taylor, C.E., et al. *Malnutrition, Infection, Growth and Development: The Narangwal Experience.* Baltimore and London: The Johns Hopkins University Press (forthcoming).

Taylor, C.E.; Faruqee, R.; Sarma, R.S.S.; Parker, R.; and Reinke, W. "Integration of Family Planning and Health Services: The Narangwal Experience." June 1981.

Socioeconomic Aspects of Fertility Behavior in Rural Botswana

Ref. No. 671-61

This study links household income, allocation of time by household members, and demographic composition, which is largely determined by fertility behavior. The project is based on time-use data and other economic and demographic information from the Botswana Rural Income Distribution Survey (RIDS), conducted with the assistance of the World Bank in 1974–75.

By studying how households of various demographic characteristics and economic endowments allocate their time and other resources to income-generating activities, such as cattle raising, crop production, and wage employment, the analysis seeks to explain the relative contribution of different household members to household income. Particular emphasis is given to the contribution of children, ages 6–15, and women.

The sex of the head of the household, the ownership of assets (cattle, in particular), and the area of land available to the household are the major household characteristics analyzed vis-à-vis the household income and the relative productivity of household members' time. Special attention is given to households headed by women, who constitute, according to RIDS, about half of the household population in Botswana.

The quantitative assessments performed are expected to lead, among other things, to a better evaluation of (1) children's contribution to household income and (2) the costs of children to the household. The schooling of children is discussed in conjunction with the returns from education in rural Botswana and, on the other hand, with children's economic activities, which determine the opportunity costs of school attendance.

All the above information, valuable in its own right, as well as in association with the income and employment policy in Botswana, will be brought together to analyze fertility behavior as a major determinant of the demographic composition of households. The output of this research program is relevant to a variety of economic and welfare policies undertaken by the Government of Botswana.

Responsibility: Development Economics Department—Oey Astra Meesook, in collaboration with Dov Chernichovsky, Ben-Gurion University (Israel); Robert E.B. Lucas, Boston University; and Eva L. Mueller, University of Michigan.

Completion date: October 1981.

Reports

The Rural Income Distribution Survey. Gaborone: Government of Botswana, 1976.

Case Studies of Determinants of Recent Fertility Decline in Sri Lanka and South India

Ref. No. 671-70

The recent decline in fertility in Sri Lanka and in the State of Kerala in south India has attracted worldwide attention for a number of reasons. The decline has been fairly rapid and significant. Between 1960 and 1974, the birth rate in Sri Lanka declined from 37 to about 27 births per thousand population; in some parts of Kerala, the birth rate fell to 22 per thousand or even lower. These declines are all the more remarkable because they took place in seemingly unfavorable circumstances. The per capita gross national product of Sri Lanka is about $200. In Kerala, it is substantially lower, even lower than the all-India average of $150. In neither area have vast amounts been spent on family planning.

Fertility declines of the magnitude observed in Sri Lanka and Kerala are virtually without precedent in such poor populations. It is in the context of these unique circumstances and in view of the potential pay-off from a study of the experience of this region, that these case studies on the determinants of fertility decline in Sri Lanka and Kerala have been undertaken by the World Bank. For comparative purposes, Karnataka State in India, where the fertility decline has been relatively small, was also reviewed.

The principal objective of the study is to understand the process of change in fertility, in order to identify and measure the impact of the factors that caused its decline in the region. Changes in marriage patterns seem to have played a major role in bringing about a decline in the birth rate in Kerala and Sri

Lanka. The study is, therefore, equally concerned with the determinants of age at marriage.

The study is based on sample survey data specially collected for the purpose from about 5,000 households in Sri Lanka and 3,000 households each in Kerala and Karnataka. The topics covered in the survey are: demography, fertility, family planning, marriage, household assets and income, and socioeconomic characteristics. In Sri Lanka, somewhat similar data were collected four years ago for the same households for the World Fertility Survey; it is, therefore, possible to analyze changes in fertility in terms of changes in socioeconomic characteristics. In Kerala and Karnataka, available data are few and the study is based mostly on the data from the surveys.

The output from the study will consist of three country reports, written mostly by staff from the collaborating institutions. Findings from these reports will be integrated into a regional report to include a comparative analysis of the determinants of fertility behavior in the region.

A preliminary analysis of the Kerala data indicated that, between 1965–70 and 1975–80, fertility has declined by about 38 percent with all socioeconomic groups, including the very poor, sharing in the decline. About 32 percent of the ever-married women or their husbands were sterilized and 31 percent of the nonsterilized women were using one of the conventional family planning methods. Increase in age at marriage contributed about 30 percent of the total decline in fertility and the official family planning program could be credited with about 40 percent of the overall fertility decline.

Responsibility: Development Economics Department—K.C. Zachariah, in collaboration with N.K. Namboodiri, University of North Carolina (consultant), and A. Thavarajah and S.L.N. Rao of the United Nations Fund for Population Activities. The project is being carried out in collaboration with local research institutions: the Department of Census and Statistics, Government of Sri Lanka, Colombo; the Bureau of Economics and Statistics, Kerala Government, Trivandrum; and the Institute for Social and Economic Change, Bangalore, Karnataka.

Completion date: The surveys have been completed in all the areas; the data have been edited, coded, and transferred to computer tape and are now ready for analysis. The analysis by local institutions will be completed by December 1981. The comparative analysis will be completed by June 1982.

Reports

"Anomaly of the Fertility Decline in Kerala: Social Change, Agrarian Reforms or Family Planning Programs?" Discussion Paper No. 81-17. Population and Human Resources Division, Development Economics Department.

Kenya: Health, Nutrition, Worker Productivity, and Child Development Studies

Ref. No. 671-73

An earlier research project "Effects of Health and Nutrition Standards on Worker Productivity" (Ref. No. 671-15), carried out in 1976-77, investigated health and nutrition factors related to the productivity of road workers, as well as the relationship of parasitic infestation to child health and growth, in certain parts of Kenya. That research indicated that both caloric undernutrition and anemia were common among road workers, and that there was some relationship to work output. Separately, it was also demonstrated that roundworm infestations retard the growth of children.

The present project, by the same group, has been undertaken to evaluate a number of possible public health interventions to address these problems. The follow-up studies, which were initiated in Kenya in January 1978 and were extended through 1980, had the following objectives:

1. Further evaluation of health and nutrition effects on the productivity of casual laborers in rural civil works. In this study, the effects of different caloric interventions on work output were to be determined in more detail. (Study No. 1)
2. Evaluation of practical interventions to improve health and worker productivity. In a series of studies, economic evaluations were to be undertaken of alternative methods of feeding and treating the workers and of the routine provision of iron and calorie-rich foods or medicinal iron to road workers. An investigation was also made of the prevalence of parasitic diseases and their relation to anemia, and an evaluation was carried out of the feasibility of routine parasitic control. (Study No. 2)

3. Surveys of health and nutrition factors in two additional areas. This investigation at road sites in two ecological areas not covered during the 1976 research was to determine how health and nutrition problems vary in different regions and, therefore, provide a better basis for planning interventions throughout Kenya. (Study No. 3)
4. Evaluation of the feasibility and effectiveness of a parasite control program. This continuation of the study on roundworms and other intestinal parasites in children was designed to maintain control in two villages, investigate reinfection rates, and evaluate the long-term feasibility of treatment that is likely to be applicable elsewhere in Kenya. (Study No. 4)

The results of Study No. 1 revealed that workers, given 1000 calories per day, had a small (4 percent) but significant increase in work output as compared to control groups given only 200 calories. The work output improvements also correlated with improvement in anthropometric measurements such as weight for height and arm circumference. The research confirmed earlier studies that anemia was a significant constraint to work output.

Study No. 2, which evaluated the feasibility and costs of different food delivery systems for road workers, showed that workers were willing voluntarily to pay for the full costs of a nutritious snack provided to them by local entrepreneurs. This study also showed that when these snacks had a high food iron and vitamin C content, they resulted in a significant rise in hemoglobin (blood iron) as compared to diets low in these nutrients. This is of particular significance in areas where anemia is a problem, and where routine administration of medicinal iron is not feasible. Other research carried out under Study 2 showed that treatment for schistosomiasis, malaria, and hookworm also resulted in a rise in blood hemoglobin.

The results of Study No. 3 revealed, as expected, that important differences in nutritional status existed among laborers in four different ecological zones of Kenya, which must be taken into account in planning national health and nutrition programs.

Study No. 4 showed that routine deworming over a period of four years on 1,500 preschool and primary school age children using local community participation was extremely popular, effective, and acceptable. Preliminary recommendations for nationwide worker feeding and deworming programs were made.

The initial objectives of this research having been completed, the primary investigators are now pursuing further development of the recommendations of the study in two areas:

1. Delineation of specific plans for alternative public health interventions in Kenya to address the problems illuminated by this research, including an evaluation of the cost-effectiveness of different forms of intervention and delivery systems, and the possible integration of the proposed interventions with other public health programs.

2. Tabulation of the child growth data obtained from the ascariasis research (Study No. 4) for possible use in longitudinal growth charts for Kenyan children.

The final reports on these and the previous studies will be completed by July 1982.

Responsibility: Population, Health, and Nutrition Department and *Transportation, Water, and Telecommunications Department*—Samir S. Basta and Clell G. Harral, respectively. Primary researchers are Michael C. Latham and Lani Stephenson Latham of Cornell University, in association with the Rural Access Roads Programs, Ministry of Works (Kenya), and the Overseas Development Administration (United Kingdom).

Completion date: December 1981.

Reports

Basta, Samir S., and Churchill, Anthony. "Iron Deficiency Anemia and the Productivity of Adult Males in Indonesia." World Bank Staff Working Paper No. 175. April 1974.

Basta, Samir S., and Karyadi, Darwin. "Nutrition and Health of Indonesian Construction Workers: Endurance and Anemia." World Bank Staff Working Paper No. 152. April 1973.

Basta, Samir S., and Latham, Michael. "The Relationship of Nutrition and Health to Worker Productivity in Kenya." Technical Memorandum No. 26. World Bank: Transportation, Water, and Telecommunications Department, May 1977.

Latham, L.; Latham, M.; and Basta, Samir S. "The Nutritional and Economic Implications of Ascaris Infection in Kenya." World Bank Staff Working Paper No. 271. September 1977.

Latham, M. and Stephenson, L. "Kenya Health, Nutrition, Worker Productivity and Child Development Studies, Final Report" (being revised for publication). January 1981.

The Economics of Schistosomiasis Control

Ref. No. 671–74

Schistosomiasis is a tropical parasitic infection victimizing an estimated 250 million people in 71 developing countries. Already one of the most prevalent water-related diseases, schistosomiasis is spreading at an alarming rate as the habitat of the intermediate host (a snail) is increasing with the development of irrigated agriculture, hydroelectric power, and fisheries. Since 1971, the Bank has directly addressed the schistosomiasis problem in 30 development projects in 18 countries.

The present study is concerned with constructing the most economical strategy of control, using drug therapy, pesticides, and sanitary water supply. It examines dynamically efficient strategies of control. With settlement of an irrigation scheme, the magnitude of the infected population, and hence the cost of drug therapy, will change. At the same time, the scale of the snail-infested water habitat will be modified by irrigation, drainage, and snail control activities. Thus, the problem is to select a method, or combination of methods of control, that minimizes the prevalence of the disease, given a budget and any prior investments in equipment, facilities, or infrastructure.

The analytical model is constructed from three modules: the first module predicts prevalence of the infection and the probable effects of control activities. In the second module, the investment and recurrent costs of these control activities are econometrically estimated. The third module introduces optimization criteria. The modules are components of a larger planning model, but may be operated independently of each other.

The model has three stages of operation. Stage one corresponds to a precontrol period in which the spread of the infection is simulated as a function of increases in snail habitat, project population, and the resulting increase in water contact. Stage two incorporates control activities, and, thus, identifies the cost-effective combination and scheduling of control activities. The third stage simulates the epidemiology of the disease, following the application of control activities.

The empirical results indicate that a strategy combining three methods of control—drug therapy, the application of pesticides (mollusciciding), and sanitary water supply—is the most effective, but also the most costly. Drug therapy together with mollusciciding is the second most effective strategy followed by chemotherapy alone, mollusciciding plus water supply, mollusciciding alone, and finally water supply alone. Sensitivity analyses with respect to different sets of parameter values of the transmission and cost modules indicate that the above ranking of strategies by effectiveness of control is robust.

From the point of view of cost effectiveness, chemotherapy alone is the optimal strategy for a control target of more than 67 cases per 100,000 population. Chemotherapy plus mollusciciding is the optimal strategy if the degree of control effectiveness desired is between 50 and 67 cases per 100,000 population. All three control methods become only optimal for programs seeking to reduce prevalence to fewer than 50 cases per 100,000 population.

Analyses of the empirical results of the study reveal that several presently widely accepted practices are not economically rational. First, as indicated above, the gains from simultaneously operating several control measures rather than chemotherapy alone are very small and as a practical matter do not justify the additional costs that they impose. Second, the collection of extensive baseline data to be used to plan intervention is not justified. The resources expended on data collection and the concomitant delay in achieving control together reduce the overall effectiveness of a program operating under the constraint of a fixed budget. Program managers should initiate case finding and chemotherapy immediately. Third, control based upon chemotherapy was found to be fairly robust in the event of temporary interruption of the program, while other methods of control were highly vulnerable. These findings argue for implementation of simple control programs using chemotherapy rather than the elaborate schemes widely employed at present.

Responsibility: Transportation, Water, and Telecommunications Department—Frederick L. Golladay and Abraham Bekele (consultant).

Completion date: November 1981.

Determinants of Fertility in Egypt

Ref. No. 671-81

This study is a data collection project that is being carried out in collaboration with the Central Agency for Public Mobilization and Statistics (CAPMAS) of the Government of the Arab Republic of Egypt and the World Fertility Survey (WFS). The project will be phased to follow the Egyptian Fertility Survey which will collect data from 8,900 women. For the second round, 30 percent of the 8,900 households will be selected and the male heads of those households will be interviewed under the World Bank project.

This data set will be one of the few having fertility data on both husbands and wives, which will make it possible to compare attitudes toward family size and contraception. In addition, economic data on family income and labor supply will be collected from the male household heads. Therefore, the data set will contain a unique combination of economic and fertility data.

While the analysis of the data is not covered under this project and will not begin until after all data have been collected and edited, it is expected to determine not only what factors are related to the preferences for large families among men and women, but also what policies can be used to encourage a reduction in family size and the achievement of smaller families through effective contraception.

Responsibility: Development Economics Department—Susan H. Cochrane and Timothy King, in collaboration with the staff of the Central Agency for Public Mobilization and Statistics, Cairo, and the World Fertility Survey, London.

Completion date: December 1981.

Health and Rural Development in Nepal

Ref. No. 672-10

This project will examine data on health and nutrition from farm families in various locations of Nepal's Terai and Hill regions. Links will be established between environmental background variables and health status, and between health and a broad range of outcomes.

One aspect of the project will be to follow the progress of children who were of preschool age at the time of a 1978 survey of farm families in two rural districts of the Terai (see Ref. No. 671–49 in the Education section of this category). Information on the children's continued physical growth and a history of diarrheal and respiratory disease will be combined with information on their cognitive development and family characteristics. This research will add to a growing literature on the relation between a child's mental and physical development. Findings of the effects of malnutrition on cognitive development and the effects of both of these on the propensity to enter and stay in school are expected to be of general relevance for policy. The enrollment issue is of particular relevance in Nepal at present, since the government plans substantially to increase participation (and particularly that of girls) in schools.

A second aspect of this research project will be to study the extent to which indoor cooking and heating fires contribute to chronic obstructive pulmonary disorders. It is hoped that this study will yield insights, useful for sector studies, on the general economic losses caused by a high prevalence of respiratory diseases.

Responsibility: Development Economics Department—Peter R. Moock and Dean T. Jamison, in collaboration with Bal Gopal Baidya, Kathleen Hebbeler, Susan Horton, Joanne Leslie, Marlaine Lockheed, Dr. Mrigendra R. Pandey and the Cor Pulmonale Project, Dr. Robert L. Parker, Rajendra P. Shrestha, Dr. Melvyn S. Tockman, Suan Ying, and other consultants.

Completion date: February 1982.

Poverty, Fertility, and Human Resources in Indonesia

Ref. No. 672-19

Between 1971 and 1976, a sharp reduction in fertility rates took place in Indonesia, mainly on Java and Bali. This is noteworthy for two reasons. First, the reduction in fertility rates took place at relatively low levels of income and social development, although these had been improving rapidly. Second, this coincided with the implementation of the family planning program. Given that the Indonesian government has set an ambitious target for further fertility reduction, two issues are of concern to it: how to maintain the momentum of the family planning program in these islands, and whether the success of the program on Java and Bali can be repeated on the Outer Islands.

This research project aims at clarifying the following population issues:

1. To understand the process of fertility decline and to project the probable future growth rate of the population of Indonesia.
2. To assess the relative contribution of the family planning program to this decline, as compared with the contribution of accompanying socioeconomic change.
3. To identify target populations with high fertility by their socioeconomic characteristics and location.
4. To identify policy options other than family planning to maintain the current pace of fertility decline.

As regards the country's socioeconomic characteristics, the poverty issues in Indonesia were identified in a World Bank report based on the findings of a mission to the country in early 1978. The report concluded that, first, the recent rapid growth of aggregate income in Indonesia had been clouded by a controversy concerning the extent to which this growth had been shared by the poorest groups. Second, it appears that urban-rural disparities in consumption are growing and that overall inequality in both consumption and income is increasing. Third, irrespective of recent changes, Indonesia faces a severe problem of poverty, with 50 million people unable to maintain the very low consumption standard of US$90 a year. This research program will, therefore, also attempt to advance the understanding of poverty in Indonesia by addressing the following issues:

1. To establish broad trends in consumption levels over time by updating the work in the report, by taking into account data that have become available in the meantime.
2. To obtain a better description of the poor in terms of various distinguishing features, such as their demographic characteristics, their consumption patterns and caloric intakes; their housing conditions, their access to social services, and their concentration by region and urban/rural area of residence. Such a description will be helpful in the design of policies to assist the poor directly through subsidies or the provision of social services.
3. To understand the difference between the poor and the less poor in production characteristics, that is, their participation in the labor force and income-earning activities and their ownership of assets. In this way, it is hoped that some of the causes of poverty and the mechanisms of escape from it will be identified.

Two major data sets will be used in the study: the second round of the Intercensal Population Survey, 1976 (SUPAS II) and the Multi-Purpose Household Survey, 1978/79 (SUSENAS 1978/79). These data sets contain household-level data on the socioeconomic characteristics of household members, living conditions, incomes and consumption expenditures, fertility behavior, and family planning practice. In addition, information at the community level, indicating the availability of family planning and other government services, will be used.

For the reseach on fertility, the initial focus will be on individual key relationships that will become building blocks for a more complete model of fertility behavior in Indonesia. To overcome the simultaneity problem inherent in the estimation of these relationships, subsamples will be used that control for other factors not under consideration in the particular relationship that is being focused on. The sample is large enough to give information on the use of the number of children born during the past year, instead of the total number of children ever born, as a measure of fertility. Multivariate regression analysis will be used.

Initially, four factors will be studied, which preliminary analysis suggests are the most relevant in explaining the number of children ever born: household income, age at first marriage, female economic activity, and knowledge of contraception. In addition, because of the large size of the sample, the effect of the family planning program will be estimated directly by considering women of identical characteristics from two similar communities, one with an active family planning program and one without it. The difference in fertility between these communities should give an indication of the impact of the program. Women of high fertility and nonusers of family planning will also be identified by their socioeconomic characteristics.

The research on the issues of poverty will develop an analytical framework that will be based on a model of household decision making concerning the allocation of household members' time, their incomes, and the consumption of various commodities, in which children appear as an argument in the household's utility function. Given this framework, the following parameters will be studied: (1) household income, expenditures, and possibly savings; (2) participation in the labor force; (3) the demand for children and family planning; and (4) investments in child education and health.

Cross-tabulations will be obtained that will describe trends in average household consumption levels over time and give a poverty profile of the poor by analyzing their demographic and socioeconomic characteristics, consumption of major categories of goods and services, housing conditions, and access to public services. Then, in order to understand why poor households stay poor or, put differently, why the slightly better-off households are not poor, some tabulations will be generated that will classify households belonging to different income classes by the activities (work and nonwork) of different household members and the sources of their incomes. Earlier work suggests that nonagricultural opportunities in rural areas may have raised some households out of poverty. If this is borne out by the evidence, the characteristics of the rural areas in which these opportunities are available will need to be identified.

Responsibility: Development Economics Department—Oey Astra Meesook, in collaboration with Dov Chernichovsky of Ben-Gurion University, Israel, and with the Central Bureau of Statistics of Indonesia.

Completion date: June 1982.

Studies on Brazilian Distribution and Growth

Ref. No. 672-21

Brazil is the world's most emphasized example of rapid, but inequitable, growth. While everyone acknowledges that rapid growth has occurred, there is little agreement on how the benefits of that growth have been distributed and, particularly, on whether the poor have gained much in absolute terms. Difficulties in the interpretation of data are innumerable; worse, in the absence of a common interpretation, there has been little progress in understanding the economic, social, and demographic mechanisms that have generated the Brazilian combination of growth and inequality.

Recognition of the important role of demographic factors, especially at the household level, in assessing the relation between growth and inequality is increasing, but much work remains to be done to analyze the interrelationships.

The recent release by the Brazilian Census Bureau of a one percent public use sample of the 1970 population census now makes it possible to pursue several questions at the household level. The tape contains data on about 910,000 individuals cross-classified into 176,000 households and 117 identifiable geographic areas in the country. Exploratory analyses of these data have led to the design of three interrelated projects that seek further understanding of the links between demographic variables at the household level and income distribution.

The first project is essentially descriptive. It focuses on a hitherto neglected aspect (because published data were not available and special tabulations were costly) of the Brazilian income distribution issue: the relation of household size and composition (age of the head of the household, age structure and work status of members, etc.) to inequality, and household responses, particularly in terms of labor supply, to the economic pressures that have been created by an allegedly unequal growth process. It will provide an allocation of labor-force members into households and describe the extent to which the low wages of individual workers are compensated for by earnings of other family members.

In part through the other two projects, explained below, the first project will make it possible to link differences in income across households to other welfare indicators, and will contribute to the definition of socioeconomic groups. Finally, it should establish a base line for comparison with the 1980 census.

The second project examines the important question of human capital formation at the household level, focusing on the schooling decision. The distribution of schooling among today's children influences importantly tomorrow's distribution of income. A key issue is the extent to which public interventions to increase access to schooling are made more or less effective by individual family resources and the capacity of poor families to use school systems. Children from poor families may be denied access to school, either because schools are not available or because they work to supplement family incomes. In this way, poverty may be transmitted from one generation to the next, unless the link between poverty and schooling is modified by public policy. The objective of the second project is to begin exploration of the relative importance of family characteristics, on the one hand, and the availability of schools, on the other hand, in determining schooling of children. The census data provide an ideal starting point for this effort.

The third project examines another aspect of the distribution of income in Brazil—infant and child mortality. An important index of household welfare in their own right, mortality differentials also raise major questions about the relative importance of policy interventions vis-à-vis social, economic, and demographic characteristics of households in poverty alleviation. The census tape provides an opportunity for examining these influences at the regional and household level.

Responsibility: Development Economics Department—Nancy Birdsall and Constantino P. Lluch, in collaboration with T. Merrick of Georgetown University (consultant).

Completion date: December 1981.

Reports

Birdsall, Nancy, and Fox, M. Louise. "Why Males Earn More: Location, Job Preferences and Job Discrimination Among Brazilian School Teachers." Population and Human Resources Division Discussion Paper No. 81-21. May 1981.

Birdsall, Nancy, and Meesook, Oey Astra. "Child Schooling, Number of Children and Inter-generational Transmission of Inequality: A Simulation." Population and Human Resources Division Discussion Paper No. 81-19. May 1981.

Fox, M. Louise. "The Adjusted Household Income Distribution in Brazil, 1970." Mimeo. Employment and Rural Development Division, May 1981.

Lluch, Constantino. "On Poverty and Inequality in Brazil." Mimeo. Employment and Rural Development Division, May 1981.

Merrick, Thomas. "Infant Mortality and Income Distribution in Urban Brazil." Mimeo. Georgetown University: Center for Population Studies, July 1981.

Policy Analysis of Fertility and Contraceptive Behavior in Bangladesh

Ref. No. 672-23

Starting in 1976, the Bangladesh Institute of Development Studies (BIDS) initiated an ambitious series of household surveys for a study of the determinants of fertility as part of the first World Bank population project in the country. These surveys were subsequently extended and combined with a study of rural poverty. The resulting data cover about 4,000 households in four contrasting areas. The data offer detailed information on the households' economic characteristics and relationships, as well as their demographic characteristics, health and nutritional status, occupations, social status, and access to services. For various reasons, including BIDS's lack of access to modern computing technology, the data have not yet been analyzed.

The purpose of this research application project is to help in the processing of these data and to produce a policy-oriented report on the socioeconomic forces influencing the fertility and contraceptive behavior of households.

Responsibility: Development Economics Department—Rashid R. Faruqee.

Completion date: December 1981.

Policy Analysis of Fertility and Family Planning in Kenya

Ref. No. 672-35

A World Bank Country Study, "Kenya: Population and Development" (July 1980), has highlighted the serious adverse impact that rapid population growth (estimated at 4 percent a year in 1980) is having on the economy. While mortality has been reduced significantly, fertility rates have remained high, and have even shown signs of increasing slightly recently.

The Bank study, however, shows that significant variations in fertility rates exist among different population groups. Among some groups of the Kenyan population, fertility has declined in recent years; among others, it has increased. In the recent past, increases were probably larger than decreases with the result that the aggregate fertility rate has increased. In the future, this may change, especially if the forces that have influenced fertility decline among some groups could be further strengthened and broadened. Kenya has been the first sub-Saharan country to adopt an official family planning program (in 1967); the program, however, has faced two persistent problems—low effective demand for family planning and the high rate at which family planning acceptors drop out.

The purpose of this research application project is to work largely with two Kenyan institutions—the Population Studies and Research Institute, and the Family Planning Research and Evaluation Division of the Ministry of Health—to follow up on the Bank study in two areas of population research.

First, multivariate analysis of fertility determinants will be conducted to provide insights about the socioeconomic forces that
explain high fertility in Kenya. This will be done by using more
recent data—the World Fertility Survey for Kenya (1979) and the
1979 Census. The research will focus on the effects on fertility of
socioeconomic variables, such as wife's education and employment, husband's education, urban residence, farm size, opportunities for child labor, women's status and role in the household and
so on. The effects on fertility of some practice variables such as
length of breast feeding and use of contraceptives will also be
studied.

Second, the reasons for the poor contraceptive coverage
achieved so far by the official Family Planning Program will be
studied. This will be done by fully evaluating data collected over
time on family planning clients. The study will focus on: (1) the
correlates of acceptance and continued use, (2) the socioeconomic
profile of those who continue to use the services and those who
drop out, and (3) causes of discontinuation by surveying those
who did not revisit on schedule. In addition to the continuous
users and discontinued acceptors, a profile will be constructed of
nonacceptors from the Kenyan World Fertility Survey.

Responsibility: Development Economics Department—Rashid R.
Faruqee.

Completion date: December 1981.

Determinants of Fertility in Egypt: An Analysis of the Second Round of the Egyptian Fertility Survey

Ref. No. 672-42

Economic models of fertility for developing countries have
evolved substantially from the simple demand models of the
1960s. It is increasingly recognized that in many developing
countries fertility is constrained by the biological supply of children rather than the demand for children. This is particularly
true in countries with high infant and child mortality and poor
maternal health. Easterlin (1980)[1] has developed a model of fertil-

---

[1]R.A. Easterlin, *Population and Economic Change in Developing Countries.* (Chicago and London: The University of Chicago Press, 1980).

ity determination explaining how supply and demand interact and jointly determine contraceptive use. This model has been applied to a number of data sets of the World Fertility Survey (WFS) and has been used as an organizing framework in Cochrane (1979).[2] The research proposed here goes beyond the earlier theoretical and empirical work by including husbands as well as wives in the determination of the demand for children and including data on income and employment as explanatory variables, which are not usually well captured in fertility surveys.

The data for testing this model have been collected explicitly for this purpose in a collaboration between the Bank, the World Fertility survey (WFS), and the Central Agency for Public Mobilization and Statistics (CAPMAS), Cairo (see also Ref. No. 671–81 in this category). The source of these data is a nationwide sample of 8,900 women and a subsample of 2,300 husbands in 100 clusters. Egypt offers an ideal environment for testing this model since other data show that there are large numbers of couples in each of the four groupings defined by the Easterlin model.

The objectives of this research are to investigate:

1. The relative importance of husbands and wives in determining the desired family size and adoption of contraception. This would permit a better targeting of information, education, and communication programs as well as family planning delivery services.
2. The effect of access to family planning services on usage.
3. The relationship between education and fertility in Egypt and the effect of school access, relative to parental demand for schooling on school participation, particularly of females.
4. The relationship between the availability of health facilities, family characteristics, and infant and child mortality and the effect of such mortality on fertility through demand and supply variables.

In addition to these policy variables, the analysis will also explore the relationship between wages and employment opportunities for women and children and fertility, as well as the effect of family income on both the biological supply and the demand for children.

[2]S.H. Cochrane, *Fertility and Education: What Do We Really Know?* (London and Baltimore: The John Hopkins University Press, 1979).

The basic model to be tested is block-recursive. The major blocks are demand for children, the biological supply of living children, and the availability of contraception. Contraceptive usage is the ultimate dependent variable. Within each of these major blocks, there are submodels such as age at marriage, income determination, child survival, and so on. The block-recursive model will also be used to organize the work. The three major collaborators will agree upon the details of the model and then will separately estimate their blocks and finally combine their results to trace through the effect of exogenous variables on the primary dependent variable, as well as secondary variables such as school participation and survival of the most recent birth.

The major output of the work will be two monographs. The first will be a descriptive report similar to the first country reports of the WFS. This is expected to be completed by September 1982 if the Bank receives the clean data by December 1981. The second report will be a more detailed estimation of the model discussed above; it will take approximately two years.

Responsibility: Development Economics Department—Susan H. Cochrane, in collaboration with Richard A. Easterlin and Eileen Crimmins of the University of Pennsylvania and M. Ali Khan of The Johns Hopkins University (consultants). The major institutions participating in the project are the World Fertility Survey and the Central Agency for Public Mobilization and Statistics, Cairo.

Completion date: July 1984.

Indexes

Country/Regional Index

Numerical Index